the SHADE BOOK

Roman
Cloud
Balloon
Roller Shades
Shade Toppers
and more

by Judy Lindahl

PalmerPletsch PUBLISHING

Dedicated to Chuck Pringle
my printer and friend for over 20 years.

Special thanks for their help and encouragement to Laurie Adam,
Marlene Bastian, Jim Chumbley, Mary Giese, Tony Picoy, Pati Palmer,
Sandy Westbrook-O'Bryant, Judith Winters, Linda Wisner, all of you
who have used and enjoyed the original version of The Shade Book and
waited patiently for this up-dated edition. I am grateful for your kind
words and friendship.

Copyright© 1978, Revised 1980, 1992, Fourth Edition 2004
by Judy Lindahl, 3211 N.E. Siskiyou, Portland, OR 97212 U.S.A.

Thirtieth printing 2004

Illustrations by Laurie Adam
Front cover photography from Waverly, 79 Madison Avenue, N.Y., N.Y.
10016 (800) 423-5881

Library of Congress Control Number: 2004117251
Published by Palmer/Pletsch Incorporated, 1801 N.W. Upshur Street,
Suite 100, Portland, OR 97209 U.S.A.
Eagle Web Press and Your Town Press, Salem, Oregon U.S.A.

Fourth Edition ISBN 0-935278-55-9

Contents

Introduction

You are about to discover the excitement and the economy of making your own shades! There are many styles and techniques from which you can choose. The easy step-by-step instructions in this book will bring you success as you discover the feeling of accomplishment that comes from creating your own decor.

Each shade may be used alone or combined with a valance or cornice, curtains or draperies, side panels or shutters. Such versatility makes for exciting decorating.

One of the best reasons to decorate with shades is that they can help save energy. (See Energy Savers.) Shades can also give protection. Installed on south or west facing windows, shades help cut down exposure to sunlight which can be damaging to fabrics and wood finishes. Shades can replace cupboard or closet doors, hide shelves and storage, conceal laundry equipment or a sewing center, serve as room dividers and provide answers to decorating challenges.

If all of these reasons are not enough to convince you that you will love your shades, there are new products and techniques that can help you save time, money and energy as you create. A world of beautiful fabrics awaits your special touch.

So get busy! Size up the situation and begin creating your own impressive professional shades.

Chapter One
Timesavers

These techniques and equipment help minimize the time and energy you expend. They are 'sanity savers' for do-it-yourselfers.

Graphing

Draw a miniature finished version of your shade, especially Roman shade styles. You can locate mounting ease, ring and pleat location, hem location and depth, rod pocket placement, slat placement, seams, splices, etc. It helps you think through the project, making errors less likely. It does not have to be perfect or to scale, but all the necessary numbers should be there. Be sure to make any notes or comments to yourself right on your sketch. Then you won't forget them later.

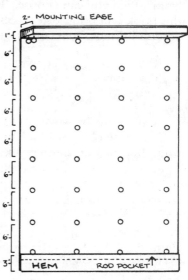

Folding Cardboard Cutting Board

The cutting board simplifies squaring fabric, backing or lining, marking the positions for pleats, tucks, rings, or slats. You can pin into it, and press on it. Easiest to use are those with a 1" ruled grid. For large shades push two boards together, or cut a second one in half and tape together.

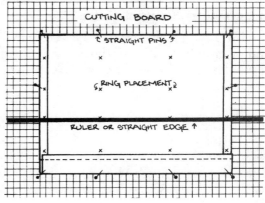

Your work surface should be large enough to support the entire shade. This means better accuracy in measuring and cutting, and reduces handling of the fabric. A 4' x 8' sheet of plywood, a ping pong table, several tables pushed together in a recreation hall or church basement may all work. Least desirable is to crawl around on the floor (terribly hard on knees and back), but it can be done.

Extending Your Carpenter's Square

One of the most important tools in decorating is the carpenter's square, available in hardware departments. It is indispensable for accurate corners — especially if you are not using a cutting board graph. Because the sides on the carpenter's square are quite short, it becomes difficult to achieve accuracy on long edges. One solution is to extend the square by slipping on a piece of aluminum U-channel available in hardware departments. The channel just fits the size of the square. It is available in 6' and 8' lengths and provides a good smooth straight edge.

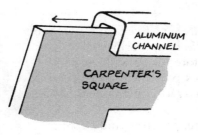

ALUMINUM CHANNEL

CARPENTER'S SQUARE

Metal Straight Edge Guides

In shade making a long straight edge is important. One inch by eighth inch aluminum flat bar in 6' or 8' lengths solves this problem nicely. It is available in hardware stores and is much less expensive than metal rulers. (It also makes a good weight bar for Roman shades.) An old Venetian blind slat makes a nice alternative.

'Decorator' Straight Pins

Use 1¾" quilter's pins, or 1½" corsage pins available from floral supply or hobby and craft shops. Extra length makes it easy to secure layers of fabric, tucks, and pleats. The ball head makes them easy to hold and to locate.

Fusibles

Fusibles are great time-savers. They allow you to bond fabrics together with an iron. Think of them as heat-activated dry glue. The old standby Stitch Witchery and other brands like it are mono-filaments of heat-sensitive fibers arranged in a random pattern. They come by the yard in 18" widths or in pre-cut strips or rolls. The webbing is placed between two fabric layers. Heat and steam are applied, which melts the webbing and fuses the fabric layers together.

Paper backed fusible transfer web is another fusible type that requires a two-step process, but the release paper makes these types easier to handle in many applications. The fusible is dry ironed for a few seconds with the paper in place, then allowed to cool before the release paper is removed. The fusible side is then placed against the second fabric and steam pressed using a damp press cloth to complete the bond. This fusible type is especially useful for appliques and craft projects.

Repositionable fusible web has a pressure-sensitive coating on one or both sides of the web, allowing you to temporarily stick this fusible on an applique, for example, before fusing with an iron. The temporary bond allows you to check placement and reposition this piece to be fused before using the iron for a permanent bond.

Most fusible webs require heat, moisture, pressure, and *patience*.
- **Heat**—iron usually set on wool
- **Moisture**—steam iron *plus* damp press cloth
- **Time**—10 to 15 seconds in each spot for a strong bond.
- **Patience!**—The reward is a perfect bond. Improper bonds may loosen in washing or cleaning, so it is worth the effort to do it right the first time. *Resist the urge* to peek and peel the fabric to see if the bond is taking. *The bond sets as it cools.*

NOTE: Because different brands have different hand, bonding strength and fusing requirements, make a test sample beforehand. Always follow manufacturer's directions on type of heat, use of press cloth, iron temperature, and bonding time.

Steam-A-Seam®, HeatnBond®, and Wonder Under® come on a release paper. These fusibles are particularly effective for appliques with raw cut edges. Wonder Under® is dry ironed for a few seconds on the paper side then allowed to cool before the paper is peeled away. The web is then placed against the second fabric and a damp press cloth is used to complete the bond. HeatnBond® release paper fusible has directions that call for dry heat only.

Steam-A-Seam® products have a release paper, and one side of the fusible has a tacky surface which allows placing the fusible with assurance it will not slide out of place while being fused. It will not gum up a sewing needle and is washable and drycleanable.

HeatNBond, a sheet adhesive on release paper, requires medium heat, dry iron and only 1 to 5 seconds of bonding time depending on fusible.

Yes, all of us will occasionally get fusible resin on our irons. The easiest way to clean it is to use a hot iron cleaner such as Iron-Off, or denatured alcohol.

Where To Use Fusible Web

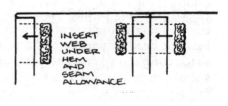

- To secure seam allowances and/or side hems before a hem is stitched. Weight rods, slats, elastic can then be inserted without 'hanging up'
- For hemming
- To attach appliques, ribbon, trims, and fabric bands
- To stiffen and strengthen fabric in hems and cornices.
- To make roller shades

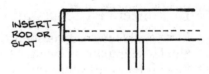

Gluing

The use of tacky fast-drying fabric glues or roller shade laminating glues can short-cut many steps in shade making. The key is they must dry flexible.

- Glue trims to shades
- Glue up a facing or hem
- Glue on a ring tape, then stitch it
- Glue — treat edges of fabric to prevent fraying
- Glue — treat knots so they won't slip or untie

Hot glue guns and the newer cool melt guns are indispensable tools in most workrooms. They can be used to apply trims, welting, secure rosettes or bows, etc.

Rotary Cutters

Razor-sharp rotary cutters make quick work of the long, straight edges for shades, linings, and contrast bands for trim. Use them with the special cutting mats designed for that use. A mat grid ruled for easy measuring is the handiest.

Water & Air Erasable Markers

These marking pens allow you to draw directly on the fabric, making them useful for marking hems, locations for rings, trims placement, pleats, tucks, and so on. Depending on the type of marker you are using, the marks can be removed by 1) rubbing gently with a well-moistened cloth, 2) using the eraser or brush tip that comes with the pen, 3) letting the marks dissolve in the air (air-soluble marks disappear in 48 hours).

Fray Check™

Dritz® Fray Check™ is a clear liquid that can be applied to edges of fabrics to prevent raveling. You may find it easier to use than the bead of glue method described later in this book. A dab on shade cord knots keeps them from coming loose. Always try a test sample on your fabric scrap before proceeding with the whole project. Fray Check™ is in notions departments.

Buttoneer® Fasteners and Attaching Tool

Small U-shaped fasteners can attach brass rings to Roman Shades, eliminating sewing. They are completely inconspicuous on most prints and gathered shades. If shades are not too large or heavy, fasteners (placed horizontally) may serve as the rings. Use very fine cord like Warm Products 1mm shade cord or Conso and Wrights .9mm cord.

Smocking, Pleating, Shirring, and Shade Tapes

Shade, valance, and drapery construction is made easier with premade drapery tapes from Europe by Conso® or Wrights®. These tapes are applied flat to the fabric, then their woven-in pulling cords are drawn up, creating the smocked, pleated, or shirred heading. The tapes are washable, dry-cleanable, and shrink-free. When sewn on, they are nearly invisible from the outside. Some versions are iron-on tapes, which eliminate the need for sewing.

Cut 'N' Tuck Cornices and Valances

Cornice products of soft, medium or extra firm foam are shaped with grooves into which fabric is tucked, wrapped and pinned. Minimal or no sewing is required. Look for products in fabric stores, home decorating departments and home workshops. (See Resources)

Quick-Change™ Foam Cornice

tuck

Velcro-front Rod

A Roman/Austrian rod from Kirsch features Velcro hook tape on the front edge. Shades, cornices, and valances with loop tape along the top can easily be mounted to this rod.

Shade Ring Repair

Once in a while a ring will break creating a problem of whether to completely unstring a shade to fix it. Jewelry jump rings, or split rings, can come to the rescue. They can be sewn to the shade, then fastened over the cord.

Wood Joiners

For those of us with less than master carpenter skills, these sharp-toothed metal fasteners are handy for building cornices and joining wood pieces. Available in hardware stores.

T-Handles

The crank handle on casement windows can be replaced by this shorter version so shade and handle do not interfere with each other.

Swag Holders

Several hardware options make swags and rosettes easier to create. Fabric can be draped across the holders, pulled through openings, and fanned out to form rosettes. Some hold multiple fabric pieces for intricate treatments, easily made.

Dowel Splices

When you can't locate dowels in longer lengths, splice them by gluing two pieces to a short length of sturdy drinking straw or plastic tubing.

Floss Holders

To quickly and neatly bundle the excess pulling cords from smocking and shirring tapes, use floss holders found in stitchery departments.

Chapter Two

Energy Savers

Shades are one of the simplest and most energy efficient window treatments. Used alone or added to an existing window treatment, shades can help achieve energy benefits by holding heat in during the winter and reflecting it in summer.

Understanding R-Value

To further understand why shades should be considered for your windows it helps to know a little about R-value, which is the degree of *resistance* to heat flow, including winter heat loss and summer heat gain. An insulated 2x4 stud wall has an R-value of about 10 to 13. A single pane of glass has an R-value of just 0.89. Double glazing yields R1.8, triple glazing R2.8, and quadruple glazing R3.7. It is easy to see that a lot of energy is literally going out the windows.

Even simple shades, carefully constructed and installed can yield an R2.0. Shades using quilted construction can achieve R4.0. Some types of Roman shades, sealed at the edges and incorporating several layers of fiber batting, have been rated from R2.5 to R5.5.

Study Reveals Savings

A study by the Illinois Institute of Technology in 1975 revealed that in summer a sunlit window with a shade admits 50% less heat than a bare window. A shade on a non-sunlit window admits 25% less heat. In winter the use of shades in a house with 15% window area reduces heat loss by about 10%. However, when the outside temperature is above 20° the shades should be raised to allow for passive solar heat gain where possible. A shade set inside a casement reduces heat loss by 25%. Hung loosely outside the recess, effectiveness drops to 10%-15%.

Another study showed that a good quality opaque (room darkening) shade can cut summer heat gain by 63%; while translucent shades cut heat by 44%.

It is important to remember that these results were obtained in controlled laboratory situations. Your home is not a laboratory. Each room and window can have variables affecting results. Just how much energy savings you can achieve with your newly constructed shades depends on the method of installation, the style or type of shade, the fabric, backing and method of construction used, and whether or not you *use* them.

To achieve maximum benefit from shades, here are a few guidelines.

Snug Accurate Mount

Shades should be mounted to fit snugly without gaps where air can flow around or under them. This means they should fit close to the window frame on inside mounts and be "sealed" or snug to the wall on outside mounts. If may mean giving up a fancy hem treatment in favor of energy savings, or adding a cornice to trap air at the top of the window.

Roller shades mounted inside with maximum 1/4" clearance on sides will be most effective. Roman shades with inside mounts are more efficient than conventional outside mounts but less effective than sealed edges.

Shade Style

Roller shades with a straight bottom that can rest on the sill to help "seal" the treatment will give maximum results when coupled with tight fitting sides and top. Roman shades that fall flat and fit snugly at sides and bottom will be most energy efficient. The goal is to eliminate gaps where air can flow around and under the shade. Folded or pleated types such as hobble shades, the softly gathered and often sheer cloud shade, and Austrian shades will be the least energy efficient.

Combining shades with other treatments such as drapes, curtains, shutters, and other shades can produce additional energy savings.

Fabric Choice

Decorator fabric and lining or backing choices have a definite effect on energy saved. Tightly woven fabrics are more efficient; sheers and open-weave fabrics are least efficient. For roller shades, the more opaque and dense the backing, the more energy saved. Therefore, blackout (room darkening) shades save more energy than translucent types. Dark colors will absorb heat—which may be fine in winter but not in summer. In hot climates, dark fabrics could cause enough summer heat buildup to shatter the glass. Thus lighter colors are preferred for shade backing fabrics. An alternative would be one set of shades for each season.

Construction Techniques

When constructing Roman shades, adding a thermal layer provides more insulation and thus energy efficiency. One option is a thermal lining, which is flexible and does not detract from the pleating action of the shade. A layer of polyester fleece inside the shade also can lend insulating value with minimal bulk.

If you need more insulation, you might consider an extra layer or two of fiberfill, or thicker layers, such as quilt battings. These add to energy savings—but also add to shade bulk. A better way to improve efficiency would be to add a layer of plastic film (4 mil) between the decorator fabric and the fiberfill layer. You want to achieve a balance between aesthetics and energy efficiency.

In shade construction, the fiber layers are cut the finished size of the shade and placed in the shade between the decorator fabric and lining. Because of the additional bulk, the decorator fabric must be cut wider to compensate. Make a small test sample by wrapping a piece of decorator fabric around the edge of your insulation layers to judge the added length needed.

The shade should fit snugly in the window opening. Some designers suggest making the padded, insulated Roman shades ½" to 1" wider than the opening to assure a snug fit.

The bulk of added insulating layers will cause the shade to be too short if you are sewing tucks or folds. To judge how much length is needed for each tuck, make a sample including fabric, batting, lining, and inserting slat or dowel if used. Release the tuck and measure it. Then add the appropriate amount for each tuck

Another modification to consider is placing the weight bar in the bottom hem edge, rather than in a pocket higher up on the shade, especially if the shade will rest on the window sill.

Chapter Three

Roman Shade Basics

This exciting window treatment encompasses a whole family of variations. It would be possible to have Roman-type shades in every room in the house — and have each room different. Fantastic!! Perhaps just as fantastic are the many new products that can make shade making faster and more creative. Different products create different looks, which is also a factor in their selection, but how fortunate we are to have these choices.

Each variation builds on the Basic Flat Roman Shade. Once you understand the basic shade, you can branch out to create interesting and exciting changes in the texture and dimension of your shades.

WHAT IS A ROMAN SHADE?

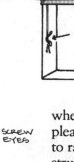

AWNING CLEAT

MOUNTING BOARD

PULLING CORDS

SCREW EYES

RINGS

WEIGHT ROD

BACK OF SHADE

The basic shade is flat when lowered and forms pleats when cords are pulled to raise it. The cords are strung through eyelets, rings or grommets attached to the back of the shade. Rings are placed in even parallel rows beginning at the top of a hem or weight bar. Cords are then run through screw eyes or pulleys on a 1" x 2" mounting board. Cords wind off on an awning cleat placed at the side of the window or may be secured with a lock pulley. A weight bar gives stability and balance to the shade.

Shades must be constructed and mounted square or they may not pull or hang evenly. Unlike a roller shade, excess fabric does not disappear when the shade is raised. Instead, it stacks up in pleats or folds which fall forward, becoming a design feature.

FABRICS

The type of fabric used affects the look of the finished shade. For the crisp look of the flat Roman, sturdy firm fabrics work best. If you use lighter weight or lace fabric, you may need to line or stiffen it to add body. Even then, the look will be different than that using a heavier fabric.

Cloud, balloon, and Austrian shades are at their best in softer fabrics that drape easily. But here, too, rules can be broken. I have seen balloon shades of moire and heavy hopsacking. However, *they require lots of hand dressing* to achieve the desired look.

Fabric must frequently be seamed to achieve needed width. If so, place one full panel in the center with equal strips at the sides, matching design as needed. Try to plan for a row of rings to fall behind a seam. Most professionals feel shades hang better and look better from the outside if they are lined. The fabric is also better protected from damage from sun and light. The decision is up to you.

PART WIDTH	FULL WIDTH	PART WIDTH

MOUNTING

How you mount your shade influences all of your measurements, so that decision must be made early. A 1" x 2" board is generally used for mounting the shade. This board may be painted white or covered with extra lining fabric if desired.

Inside Mount

The shade fits entirely within an opening. Accuracy in construction and mounting are critical, since the opening defines and outlines the shade. For energy savings, edges should touch or be not less than ⅛" from frame. Better yet, they should be sealed.

Cut board to fit inside the opening. Fasten by screws through the board into the window frame, or by fastening angle irons to the window frame. Mount angle irons toward the back of the board so they don't get in the way of screw eyes or pulleys.

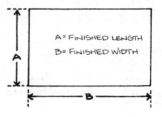

Outside Mount

The shade is installed above the opening on the frame, wall or ceiling.

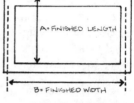

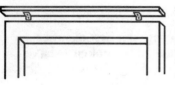

The latter allows the stacked pleats to clear the opening to give more light or clearance.

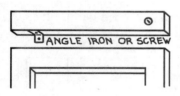

Mounting board is placed on angle irons as illustrated, or

To get a tighter fit of the shade, turn the board on edge or use a 1" x 1" board.

Hybrid Mount

Developed for use with Warm Window™ insulating Roman shade. Keeps the clean look of an inside mount while letting the shade overlap the window frame for a magnetic seal. Reduces light streaks along the sides of the shade. The mounting board fits inside the frame, but the shade is made

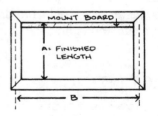

about ¾" wider on each side so the edges rest on the frame, creating a tighter seal. The bottom of the shade can rest on sill, or flat against the wall. (See construction details on page 46.)

MOUNTING VARIATIONS
Velcro Mount

A Roman shade that is mounted with Velcro is easily installed and removed. Press the top 2" of the shade (what would normally be applied to a mounting board) to the back side, and trim to ³/₄". Stitch a Velcro "loop" strip in place on the back side along the folded edge. If you use fusible Velcro, then fuse the folded-down edge in place before applying Velcro strip. Either way, Velcro "hook" tape is stapled to the mounting board's front edge.

Tension Rod

For smaller windows sew a 1½" casing along shade top. Insert a spring tension rod and fit in place at the window. Mount screw eyes in window frame above each row of rings (or in a board mounted in the top of the window). String shade, strain will be on the screw eyes.

NOTE: Mount shade on curtain rods with no screw eyes, as long as the rod can support the strain when shade is pulled.

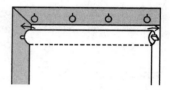

Bottom Up Shade

Secure 1" x 2" board to the window sill or floor. (Mount board toward back of sill, pleats will stack and lie forward.) Anchor two pulling cords at the sides of the shade. Two cords are threaded through the rings, then anchored to screw eyes at the top and bottom of the window frame. These are the tracking cords that hold the shade in place as it is raised and lowered.

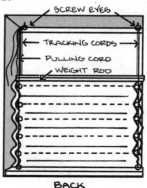

Since no cords are placed in the middle of the shade, consider dowels or stitched tucks to help retain pleat sharpness, or the pleats may need to be pressed sharply. Use a cornice or valance to conceal cords and screw eyes. This shade can be used to give the appearance of a floor length window by starting the shade at the floor.

Top Down/Bottom Up — The Athey Shade

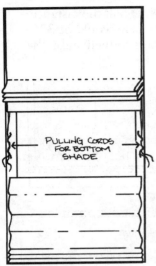

Two shades are mounted and rigged in the window so one raises from the bottom as described above, and the other raises in the conventional manner. Good on long windows or where the appearance of a floor to ceiling window is desired. The top shade serves as a

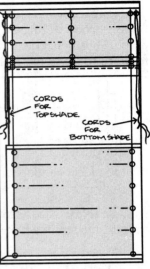

valance when it is raised. Place screw eyes for the bottom-up shade slightly behind those for the conventional shade. String one set of cords on the left window frame and one on the right.

Roller Mount

Shade is stapled to a mounting board, but cords are secured to a shade roller on ceiling brackets fastened to the underside of the board. Add at least one extra pleat length for the tug required to initiate the roller action. Use reverse roll mount. (See chapter on roller shades.)

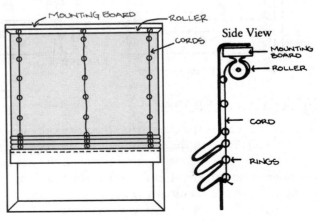

HEM DEPTH AND STYLE

The type and depth of hem finish you choose affects the *cut length* of the shade. Read through the shade directions before you start.

Standard hem depth on a Roman shade is one half the distance between rows of rings. If rings are 6" apart the hem would be 3" deep. Thus when the shade is raised, a 3" pleat is formed and falls forward to cover the 3" hem.

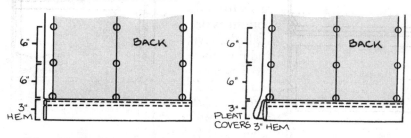

The shades illustrated in this book are based on this formula — rings 6" apart with 3" hem, unless otherwise noted.

If you want a decorative band of fabric to show below the pleats when the shade is raised, you must make a deeper hem. For example if a 3" decorative hem is to remain exposed when the cords are pulled and the shade is raised, hem must be 6" deep.

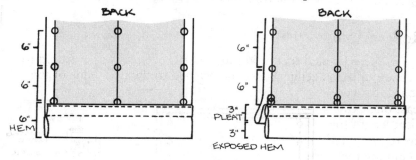

HEM VARIATIONS

In place of the standard hem already explained, you may choose to vary your Roman shade with one of the following hems. Read through the Classic Roman instructions in the next chapter, then consider these variations and make your choice before calculating fabric and cutting requirements.

Faced Self Hem

Make a self-hem as in Standard Method explained in the next chapter. To eliminate the hem strip's color or pattern from showing to the house exterior, fuse a strip of lining fabric.

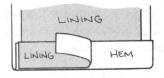

Stitched-on Facing Strip

Make the following adjustments when cutting fabric:
- Shade fabric and lining: Finished length plus 3"
- Facing strip cut from lining: 5" deep x finished width plus 2"

1. Follow steps 1 and 2 for Standard Method in the next chapter.

2. Slip facing strip under shade, right sides together. Pin even with bottom edge, with 1" extending at each side. Stitch a ½" seam allowance along the bottom edge.

3. Press facing strip to shade wrong side. Fold and press side extensions in so they do not show from the right side. Fuse the side hems.

4. Press under 1" to form a 3" hem. Stitch hem and rod pocket. Continue with steps in Standard Method.

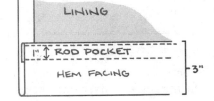

Shaped Hem

Make a deep hem treatment. Right sides together, turn fabric back on itself. Stitch hem shape, clip, turn and press. Stitch top of hem in place and stitch again to form rod pocket. As an alternative, use a strip of lining in place of the self-hem back piece for an all-white look on the shade back.

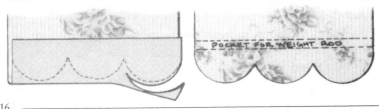

Double 2" Hem with Slat

Make a 2" double hem on bottom of shade. Insert a wood slat ¼" x 2" for weight bar (actual finished slat size is ¼"x 1½"), or use aluminum flat bar.

Separate Hem—Shaped or Contrast Fabric

1. Prepare two fabric strips 9 ½" deep x finished width plus 2". For lined shade, make one strip from lining fabric.

2. Place right sides together and stitch hem shape—starting and stopping 1" from side edge—or for a straight hem, stitch a ½" seam.

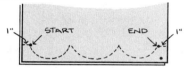 

3. Turn and press hem, clipping and trimming as necessary, so wrong sides are together. Fold the 1" side extensions in toward the center.

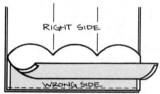 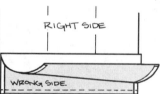

4. With shade right side up on work surface, pin hem section's outer layer to shade lower edge, right sides together. With hem facing (lining) layer out of the way, stitch a 1" seam.

5. Turn hem section down into finished position. Press. Turn shade wrong side up and fold hem facing into position. Fold and press 1" in at the top edge of the hem facing. Stitch in place (or whip by hand), then stitch again to form rod pocket.

 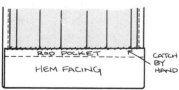

PULLING CORDS

Pulling cords should be fine, smooth, strong, and non-stretchy There is a wide variety in quality and weight on the market. If you choose to use lock pulleys, too much bulk from too large or too many cords can be a problem. If there are few cords and they are very fine, some brands of pulleys may not grip them securely.

Once the cords have been strung, and the tension balanced and adjusted, you can lower the shade and knot the cords just below the final screw eye. Or when cords are fine, simply knot the cords to a Roman shade ring.

Whichever method you choose, the cord ends may then be braided and knotted again at the bottom end, or attached to a plastic cord tassel.

The American Window Covering Manufacturer's Association reminds us that shade and drapery cords can, unfortunately, be a source of danger to small children.

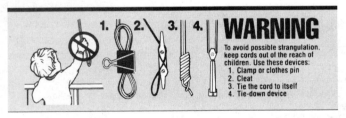

This warning tag or a similar tag is attached to products sold by members of this association.

Remember, keep cords high and securely out of children's reach.

Continuous Cording

This method reduces cord tension problems which cause shades to hang crooked. Try to use an even number of rows of rings. Start with two outside rows of rings. Run cord down one row, across bottom and up other outside row. Next do the two rows near those just strung using

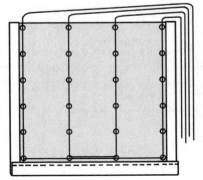

one cord in the same pattern. Continue until all rows have been strung.

To level the shade raise it and hold it level in one hand while with the other you pull the cords to tighten the tension. If you have had difficulty keeping shades level—you'll love this technique!

Fishline Threading

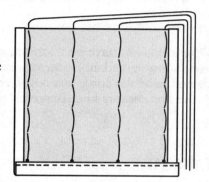

Instead of rings and cords, fishline can be sewn through the shade at intervals, run through the screw eyes, and tied off and used to pull the shade.

The line will make a nearly invisible lacing.

WEIGHT BARS

Since as far back as I can remember, Roman shade directions have called for a ⅜" brass (non-rusting) rod. Somehow that became the standard. These rods are still available, if you can find them. But they are a trouble spot for many shade makers. So it is time to think creatively. Why can't the rod be ¼"? It can. Why can't it be made from some other material? It can. For example consider:

- aluminum rod or flat bar (home improvement centers)
- a dowel or wood slat
- a piece of curtain rod
- a galvanized flat bar
- chain link fence tension bar
- a plastic plant stake
- smooth or threaded steel rod (rustproof it)
- acrylic (plastic) rods

I once took apart a very expensive custom shade and discovered a piece of concrete re-bar used for the weight bar. That's when I decided that this "sacred" weight bar can be — whatever works!!

Chapter Four

Roman Shades: The Classics

The following methods all produce a classic shade, smooth and flat when lowered. They require a minimum of fabric and show off a print or design to advantage since there are no pleats or tucks. Each method showcases a particular technique or product which gives each shade a distinctive character of its own.

STANDARD METHOD

My favorite basic method—updated; it is *fast* and *accurate*. Face fabric is prepared on the work surface, then the lining is positioned right on the face fabric, for a minimum of handling and pressing.

NOTE: Method is updated from earlier editions to make it faster by incorporating a self hem. The stitched-on facing strip technique, still a favorite of mine is found on page 16 under Hem Variations.

Measuring (after piecing)

Shade Fabric Width	=	Finished width of shade plus 3"
Shade Fabric Length	=	Finished length of shade plus 8"
Lining Width	=	Finished width of shade
Lining Length	=	Same as face fabric

1. Square grain if needed then cut, seam, and press . (A rotary cutter works very well for shade making.)   If fabric ravels easily, you may wish to use one of the following methods to stabilize side hem edges: zig zag, serge, turn under ¼", treat with Fray Check™ or glue, use a fusible .

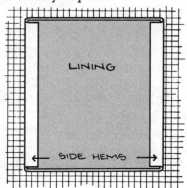

Lay fabric right side down on cutting board/work surface. Measure and mark finished width. Turn in excess at sides and press forming equal side hems.

NOTE: The fabric was cut to allow for 1½" side hems. The exact measurements may change slightly due to zig-zagging, turn of cloth, steam shrinkage or handling of fabric.

CUSTOM TIP: Custom workrooms often make side hems 2" wide. You may try both and decide which you prefer.

2. Lay lining fabric on top of shade fabric and press smoothly in place. Mark, using shade fabric as guide. Cut. Slip lining under the side hems. Smooth and press the two together. Pin shade and lining together in a few places.

Prepare 2 strips of fusible 6" long. Slip under side hems at bottom edge and fuse.

3. Fold and press bottom edge up 3"; fold and press again forming a 3" double hem.

4. Stitch top edge of hem, then stitch again 1" down to form rod pocket, OR eliminate the rod pocket and place rod in bottom of hem.

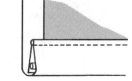

NOTE: See Hem Variations page 15 for other hem styles.

Zig zag, serge, or bind top edge of shade.

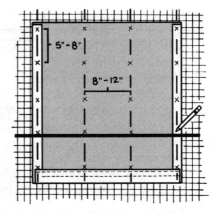

5. Realign shade on cutting board or work surface, lining side up. Mark placement of rings — keeping rows even and parallel. The first row is placed at the top of the hem and at least 1" in from side edges so rings hold side hems in place.

To mark quickly and accurately lay a long ruler or aluminum bar across the shade. Draw *very lightly* with pencil or use a water soluble or air soluble marker (see Time Savers.) Complete all lines in one direction; lay ruler in the opposite direction and make a small mark at the intersection of each line.

Vertical rows are usually 8" to 12" apart, horizontal rows are 5" to 8" apart, with 6" being the usual spacing.

6. Rings can be hand sewn in place, but zigzag stitching by machine is faster. Lower your machine's feed dogs and secure each ring with 8-10 stitches, then stitch in place a few times to lock the stitching. Without clipping threads, move on to the next ring. Sew as many rings as practical before you stop. Clip threads with a gentle touch so you don't pull out any stitches. Then apply a drop of Fray Check or glue at each ring to keep threads secure.

Reinforce the bottom row of rings since they carry the weight of the shade.

NOTE: Inserting a corsage pin or toothpick under the ring while zig-zagging creates a space or shank and helps prevent pulling or puckering on the front side, caused by tight stitches.

If you use clear thread for rings, be sure it is resistant to sunlight and watch iron temperature, as some threads are heat sensitive.

7. Cut weight rod 1" narrower than finished shade width. Insert in rod pocket.

Cover mounting board with lining or matching shade fabric by fusing (best method) or stapling. Position screw eyes in mounting board exactly above each row of rings. You may need one extra eye to help distribute the strain of the pulling cords. Staple or tack the shade in place on the top of the mounting board.

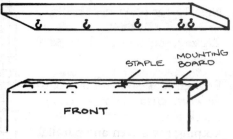

STAPLE MOUNTING BOARD

FRONT

HINT: If shade is very wide, small pulleys or roller brackets (available through drapery supply) can be used in place of screw eyes.

8. String the shade. Cut lengths of non-stretchy cord, one for each row of rings. Each will be a different length, but must go up shade and across window with the excess at one side for pulling.

9. Tie cords securely to bottom ring, thread through rings and screw eyes. Final adjusting of cords will be done when shade is in window. Put a drop of glue on the knot of each cord.

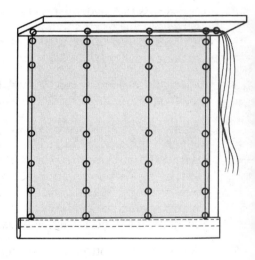

NOTE: Screw eyes at end where all cords come through must be large enough so cords don't bind up.

10. Mount shade in window. Adjust cord tension. With shade down tie a knot in cords just below last screw eye. Braid cords if desired. Mount an awning cleat at the side of the window to wind off the cords when shade is pulled. (See page 10.)

NOTE: To help train pleats, pull shade up and leave in up position for 24 to 48 hours. A drapery dressing (spray) such as Spring Mist available through drapery shops may also be used on stubborn fabrics.

SEWN LINING METHOD

Shade fabric and lining are sewn together first, requiring more handling and accuracy in cutting and stitching to maintain proper shade dimensions. This is sometimes called a pillowcase method.

Measuring
Width: Finished width plus 3" for side hems
Length: Finished length plus 9"
Lining: Length same as shade fabric minus 3"
            Width - finished width **minus 1"**

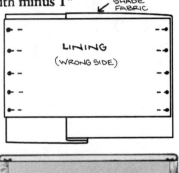
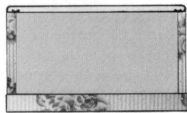

1. Lay lining and shade fabric right sides together with top edges even. Pin side edges. Shade fabric will be wider and longer!

2. Stitch ½" side seams. Pull shade inside out like a pillow-case, and press so lining is centered.

3. Follow steps 3 through 10 for Standard Method.

POCKET TAPE METHOD

This European tape and 'S' rings make quick work of Roman shade construction. The tape, which has small pocket loops woven in at intervals, is sewn to the shade, 'S' rings are inserted and cords are slipped through the 'S' ring slots. The rings are easy to insert, remove, or re-position and the slots make re-stringing a breeze.

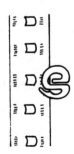

1. Follow steps 1 through 3 for Standard Method, page 20. For a custom touch, use alternate hem method, Double 2" Hem with Slat, page 17.

2. Cut Roman Shade Pocket Tape, making each strip long enough to slip under hem 1" and continue to top of shade.

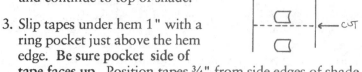

3. Slip tapes under hem 1" with a ring pocket just above the hem edge. **Be sure pocket side of tape faces up.** Position tapes ¾" from side edges of shade so tapes cover cut edge. Equally space tapes (usually 8" to 12" apart) across shade. Pin tapes and bottom hem.

4. Stitch along top edge of hem through all layers of fabric.

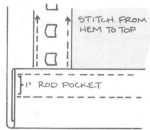

5. Stitch both edges of tapes. To prevent puckers start from bottom, reinforce and stitch toward top on all tapes.

   NOTE: As an alternative to step 5 you can zig zag just below the pockets which will hold the 'S' rings, eliminating the rows of stitching on shade front.

6. Zig zag, serge or bind top edge of shade.

7. Insert 'S' rings in pockets at about 6" intervals, depending on style and pleat depth desired. Be sure rings are even across shade.

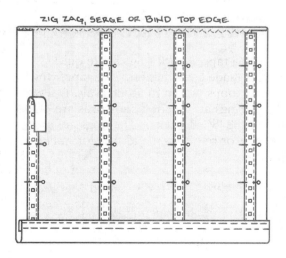

8. Wrap mounting board with lining or shade fabric. Glue, fuse or tack fabric to board. Center shade on board and staple or tack in place.

9. To string the shade first cut lengths of fine non-stretchy cords, such as Conso 1/16", or The Warm Co. 1mm cord, one for each row of rings. Each will be a different length, but must go up shade and across top of window with excess at side for pulling.

10. Tie cord securely to bottom ring. Add a dab of glue to the knot for security. Slip cords through slot in 'S' ring, then through screw eyes in mounting board.

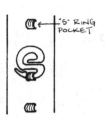

11. Cut and insert weight rod or bar into rod pocket in hem. Mount shade and awning cleat at window. See details in Standard Method.

RING TAPE METHOD

Roman ring tape has pre-spaced rings sewn to a twill tape. Tape is then sewn to the shade. It is usually considered a time-saver, not a money saver. One yard of tape contains eight rings at an average cost of $1.50 yd. Eight rings purchased separately would cost much less.

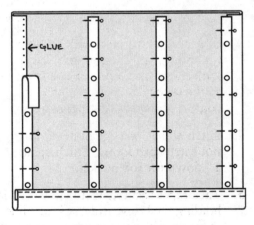

If you use ring tape, rather than stitching along each edge as the manufacturer recommends, try zig-zagging over each ring or just below it through shade and lining, to reduce chances of pulling and puckering the fabric and eliminate rows of stitching.

1. Follow steps 1 through 3 on Standard Method.

2. Cut Roman shade tapes so first row of rings starts at top of hem.

3. Lightly mark vertical position of tapes. Run a thin line or row of dots of fabric glue (i.e. Aleene's) along the lines just marked. Position tapes, aligning rings, and finger press in place. Secure with a few pins. Be sure rings on side tapes lie on top of side hems so stitching will catch hems. Stitch rings.

4. Stitch bottom hem and rod pocket. Zig zag, serge or bind top of shade.

5. Follow steps 7 through 10 for Standard Method.

LOOP TAPE METHOD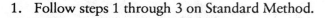

Conso or Wrights is transparent, washable, cleanable polyester tape for use on all pull cord shades. This nearly invisible sheer, strong tape makes quick work of many shade and valance projects. Cords are threaded through loops woven into the tape at 6" intervals.

1. Follow steps 1 through 3 on Standard Method.

2. Cut each tape equal to finished shade length plus 1½". Make first cut 1½" below a loop.

3. Slip tapes under hem with first loop at top of hem. Place a pin at each loop site. Place tapes on side hems so the tape just covers the hem edge. Equally space other tapes.

4. Stitch along top edge of hem; do not catch cord loops. Stitch again 1" down for rod pocket.

5. Tack tapes securely just below each loop with zig zag stitches or holding the loops aside, sew one line of stitching up the center of the tape. Zig zag top edge of shade or bind with bias tape.

NOTE: To help support the weight of large shades sew Roman Shade rings to the top of the hem at tape locations. Tie cords to rings when stringing shades.

6. String the shade using a fine, strong shade cord. Follow steps 7 through 10 on Standard Shade.

NOTE: do not thread cord through top loops if loops are less than 4" from mounting board.

TIP: Use a large needle or crochet hook to draw cords through shade loops.

FUSIBLE METHOD

With fusibles you can make a shade with no stitching lines on the front. In fact you can make a shade without sewing a stitch! Construct your entire shade, start to finish, on the work surface, using only your steam iron.

The key to success is a large work surface on which you can steam press and pin to anchor the shade as you work. Pad a piece of plywood with layers of fleece, or blankets, then cover with a sheet stapled to the back side. Whatever surface you use, it must be able to take lots of steam. A thick sheet of foam core from art supply stores, or a 1" thick foam insulation sheet from building supply (available in 4' x 8') though not as sturdy, will also work.

Measuring

Shade Fabric:	Finished width + 3"; Finished length + 8"
Lining Fabric:	Finished width, Finished length + 2"

1. Cut and press shade fabric. Lay it wrong side up on work surface. Turn and press 1½" side hems, then pin them open again. Lightly draw lines (with erasable marker) on ring tape locations.

2. Cut strips of Steam-A-Seam®, HeatnBond, or other extra strong fusible to finished length plus 2". Place on ring tape positions, even with top, 6" from bottom. (Position side strip 2¾" from cut edge, space remaining strips about 8" to 10" apart.) Iron strips to wrong side of fabric. Fuse a strip along each side ¼" in from cut edge. Let fusible cool. Remove paper strips.

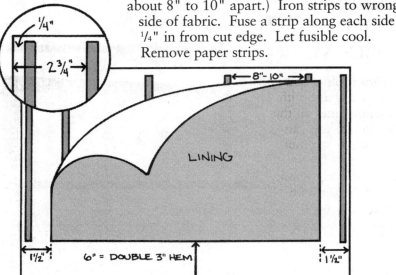

3. Center lining on fabric; use side creases as guides and place bottom edge 6" from bottom cut edge of shade fabric. Iron layers together using continuous steam on setting appropriate for lining/shade fabric. Fold in side hems; fuse.

4. Turn up and press 3" at bottom edge. Turn again and press to form 3" hem. Unfold and press strip of fusible close to fold.

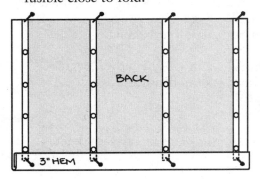

5. Cut tapes with first ring at top of hem (1/2" of tape extends under hem.). Position a row of Steam-A-Seam where each row or ring tape will lie. Press, then remove paper. Finger press ring tape into position on top of fusible and secure with a few pins.

6. Iron Tapes in place using continuous steam and applying firm downward pressure. Press around rings to avoid impression on front side. *Let cool.* Check bond. Remove pins.

7. Peel paper from fusible at bottom hem. Fuse hem. Insert weight rod or slat in bottom hem. Fuse edges closed.

8. Follow steps 7 through 10, page 26, for stringing and mounting OR follow Velcro Mounting instructions on page 15.

CUSTOM TIP: With some fusibles you may be able to heat-set the memory for pleats. Place shade on work table in raised position. Hold iron slightly above, allowing steam to penetrate. This softens the fusible. Let cool. Pleats should fold neatly without side puckers.

SWAG ROMAN

Construct shade same as for Standard Roman except put rings or Roman shade tape only on side hems. Attach fabric covered rod to top of hem.

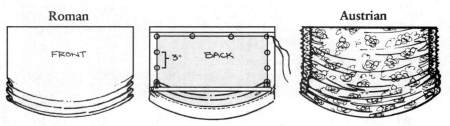

| Roman | | Austrian |

NOTE: A swag Austrian shade can be made by using Austrian tape on outer edges and making shade 1½ x to 2 x finished length. Make shade 4" wider and tuck and ease shade to mounting board.

Roman Shades: Tucked & Shirred

The methods in this chapter are made basically the same as a standard Roman shade. The main variable is that each shade adds tucks or pleats which form surface texture and sharp pleating action. To allow for the pleats and tucks additional length must be incorporated into each shade. Measurements are the same as for a standard shade with the additions or changes noted. The last three shades add width which allows for gathers and soft loose folds of fabric.

DOWEL TUCKS & SCREW EYES

This is a very smooth-hanging shade. The dowel (or slat) in each tuck lends weight and support to the shade and keeps the fabric taut. A metal weight bar is not needed because each tuck is individually weighted. Fabrics unsuited to this technique include prints whose design impact would be interrupted by the tucks and most sheers.

Measuring

To determine the additional length calculate the number of horizontal rows of rings on the body of the shade. Add 1½" of length for each row. Illustrated here 5 (rows) x 1½" = 7½" of extra length.

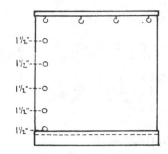

1. Follow steps 1 through 4 on standard method. Place shade lining side up on work surface.

2. Draw faint line on lining ¾" above top of hem and every 7½" on body of shade.

3. Fold and pin the shade on each line. Stitch ¾" tucks across the shade back.

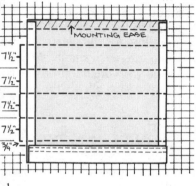

4. Slip ³/₈" dowels through the tucks. Using an awl or sharp nail, poke a small hole through the fabric into the dowel, 1" from each side edge. Insert a small screw eye in each hole.

NOTE: Instead of screw eyes, rings can be sewn to the dowel tuck.

On wide shades additional screw eyes may be needed for support.

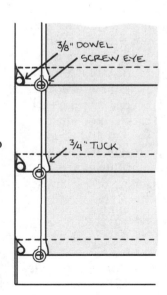

5. Tie a large knot in the end of each cord so it will not slip throught the screw eye.

6. Follow steps 7 through 10 for standard shade (omitting weight rod).

Front Dowel Tucks

Make the shade according to directions above except sew the tucks and insert dowels on the front of the shade. Sew rings behind the tucks. Make the dowels just short enough that you can close the ends of the tucks with hand stitches.

FRONT TUCKS WITH SLATS

A very tailored shade with front interest. Due to the slats the pleating action is sharp, smooth and the fabric stays taut. Front pleats create a horizontal shadow when light is behind a lowered shade. This method is suited to heavier fabrics that do not require lining, especially many lighter weight upholstery fabrics.

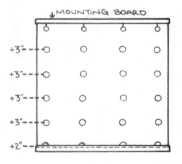

Measuring

Determine finished length plus 2" mounting ease. Calculate the horizontal rows of rings on the body of the shade and add 2" for the bottom row and 3" for all others. **This shade will have a 1½" self hem.** Rows will be spaced 9" apart.

1. Follow step one on Standard Method page 24.

2. Turn up ½" then 1½" along the bottom edge to form a 1½" hem. Stitch.

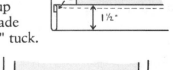

3. With right side down on work surface align and square shade. Measure up 12" from bottom edge and fold shade back on itself. Pin and mark a 1½" tuck.

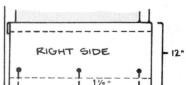

4. Continue to fold shade back at 12" intervals. Pin, mark, and stitch remaining tucks.

5. Sew rings 1" from each side edge behind the tucks and at top of

bottom hem. On wide shades an additional row or two of rings may be needed for support.

TIME SAVER: Instead of sewing rings use a Buttoneer® fastening tool to attach brass rings. The plastic stems will be hidden under front tucks.

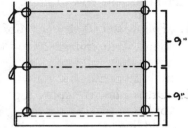

6. Insert wood slats (roller shade slats from shade shop, or thin wood strips.) Follow steps 7 through 10 on Standard Method (page 20).

FRONT AND BACK TUCKS WITH EYELETS ▬

This tailored shade pleats neatly and sharply. Optional ⅛" dowels in front tucks add dimension and keep the shade smooth. A darker line is produced by the shadow of the front tuck when light is behind the shade. It's one of my favorite methods — for the look, it stacks beautifully — and because there are no rings. Eyelets are inserted in the back tucks with an eyelet plier; pulling cords are strung through the eyelets.

Measuring

To standard length add 1½" for each horizontal row of rings.

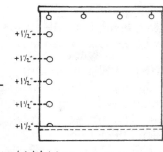

1. Follow steps 1 through 4 of Standard Method page 20.

2. Draw a line ⅜" above top of hem edge. This is the fold line for the first back tuck. Align shade on cutting board graph or work surface. Draw a line every 7½" on the remainder of the shade. (Short marks ⅜" on either side of the 7½" lines aid accuracy in stitching.) Fold and stitch all back tucks.

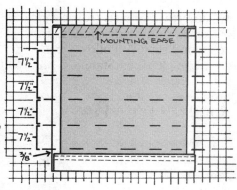

3. Fold shade back on itself, wrong sides together, pin each pleat so two back tucks are even. Stitch ⅜" front tucks.

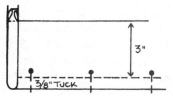

4. Mark eyelet positions on back tucks — 1" from side edges and across shade body.

5. Using eyelet plier punch holes, then insert ⅛" eyelets.

6. Insert ⅛" dowels in front pleats.

7. Knot ends of pulling cords so they will not go through eyelets. String and mount as for Standard Method.

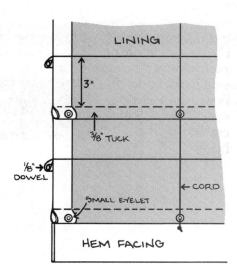

LOOSE TUCKS WITH EYELETS

A great favorite of custom workrooms. One reason may be that it can be made entirely without sewing if you use a fabric glue on the hem or catch it in the eyelets. Most home sewers will not have access to heavy duty grommet setters available through window products or tent and awning suppliers, but a little persistence with a hand eyelet plier and ¼" eyelets will yield good results.

This shade is similar to the dowel method, but the open tucks give a distinctive softened look. It is especially nice in solid colors because the tucks create a design of shadows. Some prints may not be suitable if the tucks break up the design unattractively.

Measuring

To determine additional length add 1½" for each horizontal row of rings.

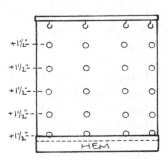

1. Follow steps 1 through 4 for standard method, but do not stitch hem.

2. Cut a strip of ¾" twill tape for each vertical row of eyelets. Cut tapes the length of the shade fabric minus 2".

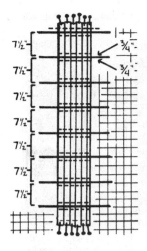

3. Pin tapes side by side to work surface. Draw a line across all tapes 1¾" up from the bottom, then every 7½" to mark the tuck locations. Then draw a line ¾" on each side of the tuck marks.

4. Lay shade face down on work surface. Slip bottom 1" of tape under hem edge, then pin tapes at center marks on each tuck—making sure the tapes are all even and parallel. Stitch top of hem.

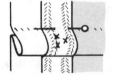

5. Pin each tuck in place using the ¾" marks as guides. Check from both sides to be sure tuck is even. Remove center pin.

6. Use eyelet pliers to punch two or three holes close together (see x's on illus.) through all layers of tuck to make a hole big enough for a ¼" eyelet.

7. Work half of eyelet through the hole in the fabric. Position other half of eyelet and squeeze *firmly* in place with pliers.

8. When eyelets are all in place, a narrow strip of molding (⅛" x ⅜") or a ¼" dowel or acrylic rod may be slipped in behind each tuck and behind side hems. Or if you like slip the molding *between* the face fabric and lining, resting on the tucks. These strips keep the shade taut and crisp.

9. Tie a large knot at the end of each stringing cord so it cannot slip through the eyelet. String and mount as for standard method.

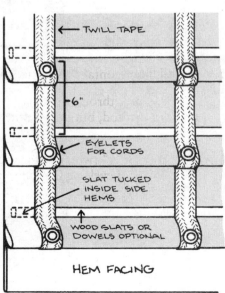

← TWILL TAPE

6"

EYELETS FOR CORDS

SLAT TUCKED INSIDE SIDE HEMS

WOOD SLATS OR DOWELS OPTIONAL

HEM FACING

VARIATIONS

Sew tuck using double stitching for reinforcement:

- If using twill tape, ⅛" eyelets can be applied to the tuck.

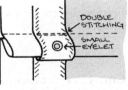

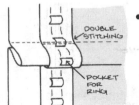

- Use Roman Shade Pocket Tape instead of twill tape. Be sure tapes are positioned so pockets are aligned across shade. Insert split rings.

- Mark twill tape as in step 3 above. Attach brass ring with Buttoneer® before sewing tucks.

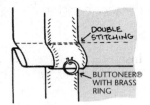

HOBBLED ▬
(Soft Roman)

The face of this shade is a series of softly folded pleats spaced 3" apart. The folds add interest and texture and hide the stitches that hold the rings in place. It is equally attractive for print and plain fabrics. Because of the narrow ring spacing, the pleats create a deeper stack up when raised than a standard Roman or the custom hobble method that follows.

Measuring

To determine the necessary length, multiply times two.

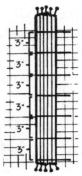

1. Follow directions for Standard Method steps 1 through 3.

2. Cut ¼" twill tapes for each vertical row of rings. Cut each tape the finished length plus 2".

   Pin tapes to work surface. Mark across tapes ½" up from bottom, then every 3" (or half the distance between the rings on the shade.)

3. Insert tapes under edge of top hem then stitch hem, catching tape. Stitch again 1" down to form rod pocket.

4. Pin each mark on tape to a corresponding ring mark on the shade, drawing up slack in pleat and forming a fold.

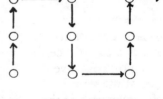

5. Place ring on pin and zig-zag over ring. Be careful not to catch extra fabric in stitching. Do about three rows at a time, using a pattern similar to the one at right. This seems to work best and wastes the least thread. Stop and clip off

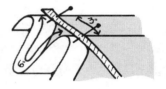

   threads, then continue with next three rows. Lay shade flat and add a dab of glue or FabriCheck (seam sealant) to seal the clipped ends.

6. String and mount shade same as for Standard Method.

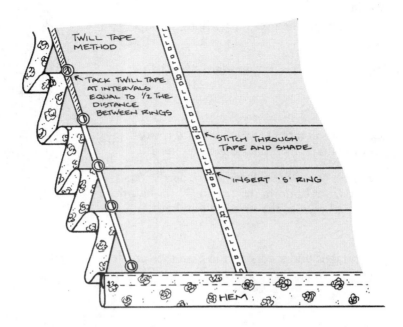

TWILL TAPE METHOD

TACK TWILL TAPE AT INTERVALS EQUAL TO ½ THE DISTANCE BETWEEN RINGS

STITCH THROUGH TAPE AND SHADE

INSERT 'S' RING

HEM

CUSTOM HOBBLE

Workrooms often make hobble shades with rings spaced farther apart, deeper hem, and wider side hems. In the following example rings are spaced 6" apart with 10" of fabric between rings. An 8" hem is used at the bottom. The resulting shade has:

- Fewer pleats (less labor intensive)
- Fewer breaks in design (less busy to the eye)
- Less bulky stack up (good on long windows)

Measuring

2 x finished length plus 10". This amount includes 4" for a "mock pleat" near mounting board, and 8" hem.

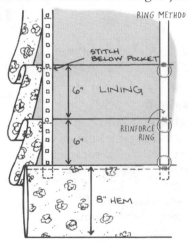

1. Cut seam and press fabric, keeping it square. Measure and mark finished width. Turn excess into equal side hems (approximately 2").

2. Turn and press 1" along bottom edge, then turn and press an 8" hem. Mark shade every 10" from top of hem to top of shade.

3. Cut Roman shade ring tapes finished length minus 6". Make first cut above a ring and measure from there.

4. Pin tapes to cutting board, aligning rings. Mark across tapes 1" up from bottom (just below ring), then every 6".

5. Slip the bottom 1" of the tapes under the hem so the ring is just above the hem edge. Pin each tape mark to a corresponding mark on the shade back.

6. Stitch hem. Double stitch tapes and shade at each ring site. Zigzag, serge, or bind top of shade.

   NOTE: If using twill tape and rings, zigzag over the ring at each location.

7. Insert weight bar in bottom of hem. String and mount as for standard method.

CUSTOM TIP: Lay wood slats in fold of pleats to give stability.

SHIRRED ROMAN

Although Roman shades are usually trim and tailored, this version is gathered, soft and feminine. It is at its best in sheer, soft, lighter weight fabrics. Extra width is gathered onto wooden dowels to create this style. Be advised that in some fabrics the gathers will require hand dressing when the shade is raised to look their tidy best. The shade will pleat easier if unlined, but lined versions are possible.

NOTE: Any gathered shade is a candidate for a shirred (or smocked) heading tape. Just a few straight lines of stitching and pulling on the cords. See Heading Variations.

Measuring

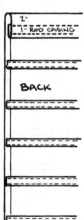

    Length: Finished length + 8 "
    Width: 2x fullness for most fabrics and if lined, 3x for sheer.

1. Press and stitch double ¾" side hems.

2. Turn and press 1 " along top edge, then 3" to form top hem. Press a double 2 " hem at the bottom edge.

3. Stitch top hem, then stitch 2 " from fold to form casing. Stitch bottom hem.

4. Lay shade on work surface and mark locations for casings. Make casing strips from color coordinated 1 " wide bias tape or self fabric strips (fuse or stitch raw ends under) or use lengths of Pocket Shade Tape (sear ends with flame to prevent raveling.)

5. Pin casing strips in place across the shade, then stitch in place.

A. Bias or self fabric casings　　**B. Ribbon Tubing**

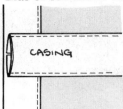 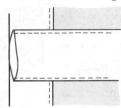

6. Cut ⅜" dowels 1" shorter than finished shade width. Insert dowels in casings and gather shade to size — distributing gathers evenly. Use staples or small tacks to anchor fabric to dowel so it will not shift. Another alternative for anchoring the fabric is to sew through casing and around dowel, taking care not to let stitches show on front (hide them in the gathers). Tack ends of casings closed.

NOTE: Dowels may be encased in lining fabric or ribbon tubing. Then you can stitch into the casing to anchor rings and stabilize gathers.

7. Stitch rings to back of shade (approx. 24" apart) and string as for Standard Roman page 23.

For Pocket Tape, omit rings and thread fine cord through the pockets.

　Stringing Variation: String every other pleat. This puts dowel on pleat edge.

Heading and Hem Variations

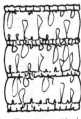  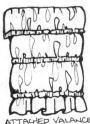

TOP CASING/　　MOUNTING BOARD　　ATTACHED VALANCE
HEM CASING　　RUFFLED HEM　　RUFFLED HEM

Shade Body Variation

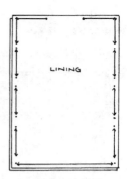

- Shade may be self-lined using a double fabric layer or fabric and lining. This eliminates the need for separate casings. Lay fabrics right sides together and stitch around all sides, leaving 1" opening along the side seams where the casing will be stitched and a larger opening at the top. Turn shade right side out, press, and and stitch top opening closed. Mark stitching lines for casings, and stitch. Insert dowels.

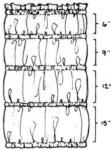

- Create graduated pleats rather than equal size. A friend who makes custom shades loves this style and thinks the graduated pleats stack batter.

  IDEA: Try a Roman shade with graduated pleat spaces for a new look!

SHIRRED HOBBLE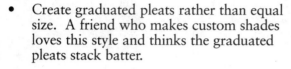

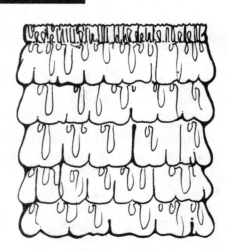

Soft folds are displayed whether the shade is up or down.

Construction is basically the same as for shirred Roman with length taken up in a hobble. Illustrated here with 4½" rod, 12" between rings on fabric, 6" between rings on twill tape.

Length: 2x finished length
Width: 2x fullness, 3x for sheers

Variation One

1. Press and stitch double 1" side hems. Press down ½" then 5½" to form top casing. Press 1" double bottom hem. Stitch top and bottom hem.

2. Cut hobble strips of ¼" twill tape (or shade tapes such as Conso) equal to the number of rows of cords, 18"-24" apart. Cut 1" below first ring location, then mark every 6" for pleat spacing.

3. Place shade on work surface and mark ring locations starting 6" up from bottom hem, then every 12". Follow steps 4 and 5 for Shirred Roman. Pin hobble tapes to the bottom casing and stitch securely in place through casing stitching lines. The strain of lifting the shade is located here.

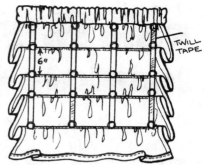

4. Pin each hobble tape to the back of the shade at ring locations, matching the 6" marks to the top row of stitching on the casing. Stitch ring and tape.

5. Follow step 6 for Shirred Roman for cutting and inserting dowels. String and mount shade (See Standard Roman).

Variation Two

1. Prepare a piece of lining to lie flat behind the shade. Allow for casing or heading, then divide space by number of 6" hobbled pleats needed.

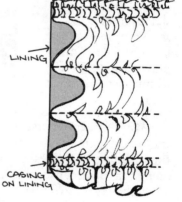

2. Prepare face fabric with double 1" side and bottom hems, and desired top heading.

3. Mark fabric every 12" starting 6" from bottom edge and continuing to heading. Stitch narrow shirring tape across back of shade (or zig zag over cord) on marked lines. Pull cords, drawing shade up to finished width. Secure cords.

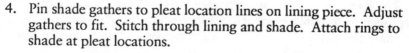

4. Pin shade gathers to pleat location lines on lining piece. Adjust gathers to fit. Stitch through lining and shade. Attach rings to shade at pleat locations.

5. Insert weight rod in bottom hem casing. String and mount as for Standard Roman shade.

   NOTE: This flat lining technique can be used for a plain Hobble, too. The street side is smooth and flat.

Roman Shades: Insulated

One of the most attractive, effective, and simple to make insulating shades available is the Warm Window® Insulating Roman Shade System. Properly constructed and mounted, these shades have been shown to reduce heat loss up to 81% and prevent up to 79% of summer solar heat gain.

Warm Window insulating fabric includes four layers channel quilted at 4" intervals. You select the face fabric, which becomes the fifth layer. Besides its energy efficiency, Warm Window has gained favor because its channel stitching helps reduce bulk, prevents the layers from shifting, and serves as the location for the horizontal ring placement, thus saving time and labor.

The fabric, which is available in 47" and 60" widths, is only one part of a system which also includes special mounting techniques and magnetic strips in the shade's edges and on the adjoining wall or window frame. In the lowered position the magnets form a tight seal, to drastically cut heat loss or gain. In the raised position the magnets create a crisp look—even in this slightly bulky fabric. To complete the seal a magnetic strip may also be placed across the bottom edge, or if no magnet is used, the shade must touch the window frame or wall in a friction fit to complete the seal.

NOTE: Channel quilting is run horizontally across window (called railroading) with a full 4" channel at bottom edge. One width of 47" fabric will make shades up to 43" tall. If finished length is over 43", you will need the 60" width or splice the 47" material.

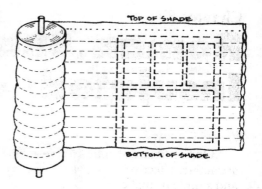

MOUNTING

Warm Window® shades can be mounted in either of three methods (see also page 11-12):

- Outside Mount - also recommended for sliding doors so all folds can raise above the window

- Inside Mount - requires more accuracy of fit and may need special moulding for the magnetic strips

- Hybrid Mount - sides overlap the frame by ¾" (maximum 1½") on each side to cover the magnetic tape. Often used on windows that are not square, where an inside mount would not be possible.

STACK UP

This is the space that pleats occupy when the shade is raised. If you want as much light as possible to come in your windows—an outside mount set on the wall above the windows would be the best choice—so the pleats clear the glass area entirely.

To Estimate the Stack of Your Shade When Drawn Up

Length of Shade	Stack Depth	Stack Width
3ft.	7"	4½"
4ft.	8"	4½"
5ft.	9"	4½"
6ft.	10"	5"
7ft.	11"	5"
8ft.	12"	6"
9ft./more	14"	6"

Measuring

Decorative Fabric – sturdy, medium weight so magnets will attract through the fabric

Width: Finished width + 3" for side hems

Length: Finished length + 12" of which 4" is for mounting ease and 8" for double 4" hem

Warm Window®

Width: Finished width of shade

Length: Finished length + 4". Be sure that a full 4" channel falls at shade bottom

Magnetic Tape

3½" Tape: Finished length x2, for shade

Unscored Tape: Finished length x2, for window frame

Bottom width of window sill x2, if you plan to magnetize the bottom edge

SPECIAL NOTE: For shades that rest on sill add ½" of length to assure a good seal. Because shade width can be affected by humidity, handling, and hanging—some workrooms add ⅛" for each foot of width over 3ft. The main thing is to measure accurately and check the measurements periodically during construction to be sure they are maintained.

CONSTRUCTION — Read Completely Before Starting Shade

1. Cut, seam and press decorative fabric. Keep fabric square and match design as needed.

2. Prepare insulating quilted fabric, splicing where needed for length.

    To splice Warm Window, cut fabric 1" from channel stitching and trim out excess bulk. Then place smooth lining sides together, meeting the channel stitching lines. Baste and check for accuracy. (Or you may pin or use a desk stapler to hold layers.) Use a standard stitch length to sew through the channel stitching. Trim seam to scant ¼". Remove pins or staples. Finger press seam.

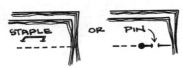

3. Pin right sides of fabric and lining together with top and side edges even. (Shade fabric will be larger.)

4. Stitch ½" side seams. To reduce edge bulk zig zag the fabric edges, catching all layers. Turn shade right side out to be sure length and width are correct. Turn extra bottom fabric up into a 4" double hem and pin in place. Recheck shade and window measurements.

   NOTE: If face fabric is not taut and smooth, turn shade inside out and stitch ⅝" seam allowance. (Do not remove the ½" stitching.) Check shade again. Face fabric should be snug, but not so tight it causes the edges to curl.

5. Place a pin at each channel stitching location.

6. Strips of peel and stick flexible magnet are used on side seam allowances. Since magnets have polarity, all strips **must be** aligned in the same direction or some will repel instead of attract. Select one of the following types of ½" magnet.

   a. Flat strips in pre-cut packs with rounded corners and one notched end. (Best—they have not been rolled.)

   b. Magnet embossed with arrows, scored to snap apart in 3½" segments.

   c. Spray paint one edge of a roll of magnet. Cut 3½" strips, nip corners. Position so painted edge is always on same side.

7. Peel backing from magnet strips exposing the adhesive. Center strips, one per channel, on seam allowance with markings in same direction. No magnet in mounting ease and none on last 4" of quilted fabric. Bottom strips are placed on **right** side of decorator fabric seam allowance just below the bottom edge of the quilted fabric. The bottom 4" have no magnet strips.

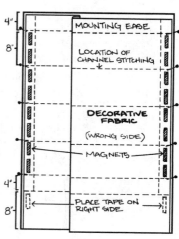

NOTE: If possible plan a row of rings to fall just below the mounting board. It holds shade in and keeps it from "poking out" revealing mounting board when shade is raised.

8. Turn the shade right side out. Press with cool iron if needed. Fold decorator fabric up to form double 4" hem. Taper side edges slightly so they don't show. Add magnetic strip across bottom (optional) on wrong side of decorating fabric.

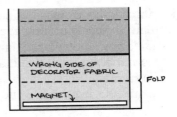

9. Choose one of the following hem finishes:
   a. **Magnetic Tape in Hem**—With magnetic tape already applied across the bottom as in step 8 above, fold a double 4" hem, aligning the fold with the channel stitching lines. Make sure the shade is square at the lower edge; adjust if needed. Machine stitch hem edge. Stitch again 1" down to form rod pocket 3" above lower edge.
   b. **Steel Bar in Hem**—Calls for magnetic tape on windowsill or wall but not inside shade hem. Cut bar to fit inside hem. Smooth cut ends or wrap with the tape. Paint or varnish bar to prevent rusting. Stitch 1" rod pocket at *bottom* of finished 4" double-fold hem.
   c. **Aluminum or Steel Bar in Hem**—Does not use magnets. Aluminum makes a good weight bar, but will not magnetize to complete the seal. Use a friction fit—shade touching sill or wall. Stitch 1" rod pocket.
   NOTE: Insert bar and tack ends closed after shade is mounted.

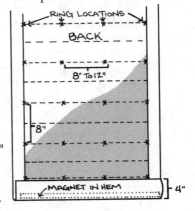

10. Lay shade flat, start at top of hem and mark ring locations 8"-12" apart on every other row of channels. Place outer rows about 1½" from edge, clearing frame and magnets.

Pin through all layers at ring locations; pin horizontally through channel stitching. Sew rings by hand, zig-zag using button stitch on machine, or use Buttoneer®. **Reinforce bottom row of (weight bearing) rings.**

11. Mount shade according to the mounting style you selected. Cut mounting board to proper length. Paint or wrap board with lining or muslin if desired. Fusing or gluing fabric to board allows screw eyes to go in without pulling and twisting fabric. Drill holes in board slightly smaller than screws.

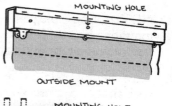

OUTSIDE MOUNT

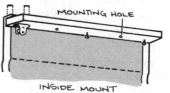

INSIDE MOUNT

Staple shade to board. Re-check for correct length. Trim off extra top fabric to reduce bulk.

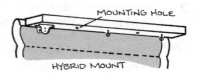

HYBRID MOUNT

For hybrid mount select one of the following mounting techniques:

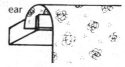

a. With the shade right side against the mounting board, align top edge of shade with front edge of board and staple in place. Staple a strip of thin cardboard across the fabric for strength. Flip shade forward and down. **TIP:** Lift shade and tack "ears" that extend over the outside of the frame after stringing and mounting.

b. Fasten Velcro hook strip to edge of board. Sew Velcro loop to top wrong side of shade. (Folded down top edge; trim off extra mounting ease.

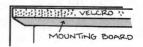

12. String shade. See steps 8-10 on page 23. Mount shade; add awning cleat (or use lock pulley.)

BACK OF SHADE

NOTE: To install lock pulley, place it above outer row of rings. Use screw on inner end and screw eye on outer end, lining up screw eye with outer row of rings. The cord next to the edge of the shade goes through the screw eye, not the pulley.

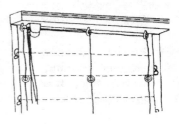

13. Measure and cut two long side strips of magnet. Set the strips on the shade to check the polarity lineup. If the magnet's edges are not even with each other, turn the long strip end to end. Leave magnets in place.

    Use alcohol to clean the wall or window frame surface where the magnets will be attached.

    Position the shade at the window. Peel 2"-3" of the paper from the magnet and seal to the frame or wall. Continue removing paper and sealing as you go. Smooth the magnet firmly in place to remove air pockets. (Try rolling with a rolling pin or wallpaper seam roller.) Magnet tape may be painted with a light coat of enamel or latex if desired.

14. To raise the shade release the seal at the bottom or side. A small pull tab or brass ring helps protect the shade from soiling. Then pull cords. The pleats may need some hand shaping until they get a memory of their own. Try leaving the shade up for 24-48 hours and/or with shade raised lightly iron over the folds with a low iron setting without steam.

Daily Use

Raise shades daily. The efficiency gained from solar radiation during daylight hours will help reduce heating bills. Raising shades daily allows condensation to evaporate and keep sills and shades dry.

Cleaning

Vacuum shades regularly to prevent dust build up. A spray-on and vacuum-off upholstery cleaner may be used. If the shade is ever to be dry-cleaned, make the following change during construction: Lay a strip of Steam-A-Seam across the top of the row of magnetic strips before the shade is turned right side out. After the shade is otherwise completed, iron the cover fabric at the edges on top of the magnetic strips. The Steam-A-Seam2® bond will hold even during cleaning. Gentle washing (dipping) is possible if cover fabric and Warm Window™ were both pre-washed before assembly. After any washing or cleaning, spray both sides with Scotchguard™ or another stain resistant product.

Chapter Seven

Cloud Shades:

The softness of this shade combined with its ease of construction has made it a favorite of decorators and do-it-yourselfers alike. A cross between a balloon and an Austrian, the cloud adapts well to many fabrics — from soft sheers and laces to crisp chintz and moire. It may be left unlined (softer) or lined (crisper) to protect fabric and preserve uniformity. Crisp fabrics will demand more hand dressing if you are a perfectionist about how gathers fall.

This shade has many faces. Seemingly endless variations are possible by making changes to one or all three of the following:

Headings - Shirred or smocked with special tapes, gathered onto rods of various widths and diameters

Hems - Either plain or ruffled

Stringing - Vary cord spacing or eliminate some cords

HINT: Collect pictures of shades that appeal to you. Soon you will be able to tell just which techniques were used as you plan your own shade. Most cloud shades can be made in a shorter version for a window topper valance.

Basic Cloud

This illustration uses soft cotton 4-cord shirring tape which is commonly found in fabric stores.

Measuring

Length: Finished length + 15" to 30" for shade with permanent "pouf" when lowered (This shade requires 24": 2" for hem, 4" for heading, 18" for permanent poufs.)

Width: Finished width x 2 for most shades, x2½ or x3 depending on weight of fabric or style of shirring or smocking tape

Rings: Sew individual rings or use ring tape.

1. Match fabric design and seam if necessary to achieve desired width. Use French seams on sheers, or serger if preferred.

   French seams: Place wrong sides of fabric together. Sew ¼" seam. Press seam flat to one side and trim to ⅛". Put right sides together, press. Stitch ¼" seam. This encloses the raw edges and prevents raveling. Press.

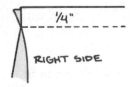
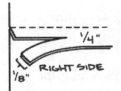

2. Turn, press and stitch 1" side hems. Make a 1" double hem on the bottom.

3. Turn down top edge 4". Lay 4-cord shirring tape in place ¼" down from top folded edge. Stitch just above and below each cord (8 lines of stitching.)

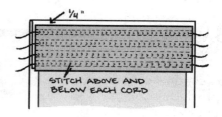

¼"

STITCH ABOVE AND BELOW EACH CORD

4. Stitch rings in place ¾" in from side edges, one at the top of the hem and one just below the shirring tape. Stitch the remaining rings equally at spaces of 6" to 10". The horizontal rows will seem very wide, but will be half that distance apart when the shirring tape is gathered

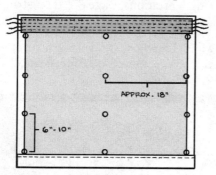

APPROX. 18"

6"- 10"

5. Tie knots in the ends of the shirring cords so they can't pull out, then pull cords — drawing up shade to finished width. On an outside mount, plan for shade to go around the ends of the board.

6. Prepare a piece of lining fabric 4"x finished width of shade. Fold in half lengthwise to form a 2" strip. Zig-zag or finish edges and ends, then tack the strip to the top of the shirring tape to form a flap that can be attached to the mounting board, OR staple through the heading into the front of the mounting board, hiding the staples in the gathers.

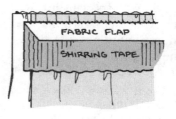

FABRIC FLAP

SHIRRING TAPE

7. Cut a ⅜" rod for weight bar; smooth ends. Cover rod with matching fabric or ribbon tubing. Fabric may be sewn, fused or glued to the rod.

Insert rod into the hem, gathering the shade's fullness to fit. Tack rod cover to hem to keep fabric from sliding about. OR Mark rod at finished ring locations. Adjust shade fullness to fit rod. Tack rod below rings at top of hem, or insert through rings. (See illustrations page 67.)

8. To create the poufs at shade hem, knot the bottom four rings together with a secure knot.

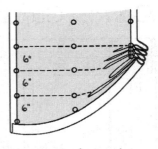

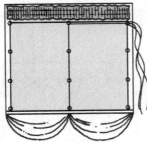

9. Read steps 7-10, page 23, and Mounting Variations, page 68, then string and mount shade.

NOTE: To adjust shade length tie up one more pleat or loosen bottom pleats.

CUSTOM CLOUD

The custom cloud includes a permanent five pleat pouf at the bottom edge, wider side hems and bottom hem and deeper (10" pleats). This is a favorite of many workrooms.

The heading may be one of the many special shirring or smocking tapes, or it may be gathered onto a rod or pole. The sample in the following directions uses a 4" smocking tape heading and Conso or Wrights Transparent Roman Shade Tape. (You may use individual stitched rings if preferred.)

Position tapes and rings so they fall on a seam and equally in between.

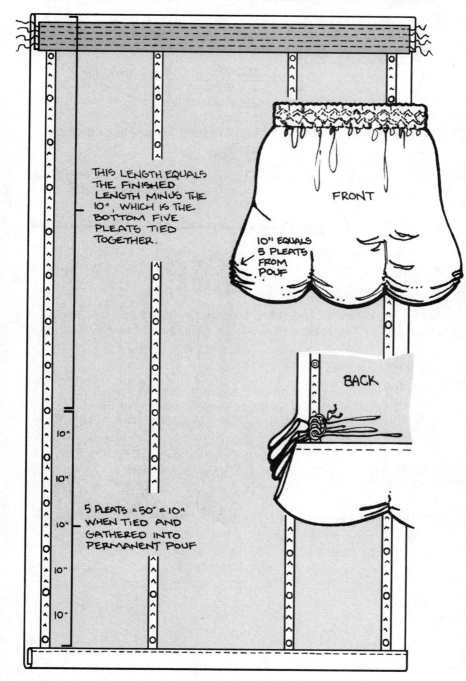

THIS LENGTH EQUALS THE FINISHED LENGTH MINUS THE 10", WHICH IS THE BOTTOM FIVE PLEATS TIED TOGETHER.

FRONT

10" EQUALS 5 PLEATS FROM POUF

BACK

10"

10"

5 PLEATS = 50" = 10" WHEN TIED AND GATHERED INTO PERMANENT POUF

10"

10"

10"

Measuring

Length: Finished length + 60"

Width: Usually double fullness. If using a special shirring or smocking tape fullness may be 2½ or triple.

1. Cut, seam, press fabric to custom cloud length and width.

2. Turn under double 2" side hems. Press.

3. According to style of heading or type of tape you are using, prepare the heading. For this example using 4" smocking tape, press a 4 ¼" hem. Cut tape wider than finished width, and fold under 1" on each end. Free the strings, ready for gathering. Pin tape in place ¼" down from top and ¼" from sides.

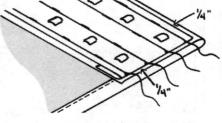

4. If you are sewing individual rings, go to next step. Cut lengths of Conso Transparent Roman Shade tape and insert under bottom hem (be sure a ring is just above hem), pin. Pin tape up shade and insert under top hem edge.

5. Stitch bottom hem and smocking tape (see page 71). Stitch shade tapes on each side (always stitch bottom to top) or, if preferred zig zag just below ring every 10".

   OR If using individual rings, mark locations and handstitch or zig zag rings in place.

OR

ZIG ZAG

6. Tie secure knots in ends of header tape, pulling cords so they can't pull out.

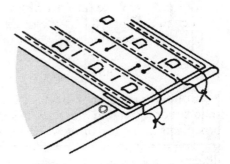

Anchor cords securely, then pull up shade using both hands to pull and push pleats into place. Adjust pleats or tucks until you are satisfied. Tie off cords. Knot securely. Add a dot of glue to knot. Trim off excess (or bundle and retrain so you can release for cleaning.)

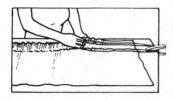 

7. Staple to mounting board by peeling fabric forward and stapling into top of smocking tape. Re-adjust fabric.

8. Insert 2" x ¼" finished wood slat or weight rod into hem. Adjust gathers, tack ends closed. Tie bottom five pleats into permanent poufs.

"BALLOON" CLOUD

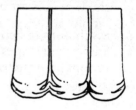

To give the cloud shade a closer family resemblence to the balloon shade, yet maintain the easy construction, eliminate casings or tapes and make box pleats along the heading instead of gathers. Create permanent poufs by tying at least three bottom pleats.

Measuring

Width: Double finished width
Length: Finished length plus 24" or according to number of pleats tied permanently at bottom edge

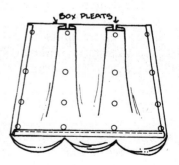

Follow construction for Basic Cloud shade. For mounting fold equally spaced box pleats at the top of the shade before stapling to the board. Pleats should be directly above the rows of rings.

QUICK CLOUD

A casing top cafe curtain can be quickly converted into a cloud shade or valance by adding rings, cords and weight bar. Mount on existing curtain rod. If rod cannot support the strain of pulling, screw eyes should be mounted in top of window frame or in board mounted behind or below rod (page 68). This is especially effective for curtains too long for the window. Tie up the excess in permanent poufs! Fast, easy, economical!

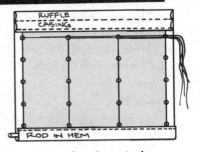

ARCH TOP CLOUD

As beautiful as they are, arch-top windows create a dilemma for many homeowners and designers because they are definitely a challenge to dress.

If you are planning a shade or valance using a casing top, the casing should fit the rod snugly, or gathers can slip down the rod after it is installed. The rod will need some support at the center top, and perhaps elsewhere. Screw eyes can be mounted on window frame or a board mounted across the window.

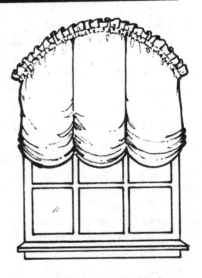

Several arch-top rods are on the market, designed to fit inside the arch or outside above the window. Kirsch has a round rod of polycarbonate that fits on barrel brackets, Graber offers a 2½" or 4½" Dauphine style. A foam-covered flexible rod is another possible choice.

Creative do-it-yourselfers have used hula hoops or plastic tubing. Some have even bent solid rods by clamping them in a vise and alternately bent and reclamped as they moved the rods along. Foam pipe insulation can be used to "fatten" a slim rod and make the fabric cling without slipping.

Method One - Straight Top

The easiest way to make this shade is to use a curtain with a straight casing top. Because the hem will be drawn up into a bow shape mirroring the arch top, fabrics should be plain colors or all-over design with no specific crosswise detail.

Measuring

Length: From top of rod to desired length add for casing, ruffle, and double hem, (and permanent poufs.)

Width: 2½ x to 3x fullness

1. Prepare fabric seaming for width if necessary. Turn, press, and stitch double 1" side hems. Press and stitch top casing (including ruffle if desired) to fit rod.

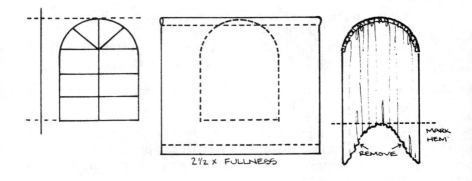

2½ X FULLNESS

2. Slide curtain onto rod and hang at window. Adjust gathers. Allow curtain to hang at least overnight. Then mark finished hem, add 2" for l" double hem and cut off excess "tails," remove from rod and make bottom hem.

    NOTE: Because a straight casing has been threaded on a curved arch, the gathers in the fabric may not fall smoothly in vertical folds. You may need to steam them or use a fabric spray wrinkle releaser to encourage this shape.

3. Mark ring or shade tape locations along side hems and equally spaced across shade. Sew rings or tapes as for standard Roman. Insert a weight rod in the bottom hem.

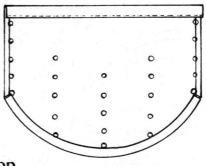

4. Mount and string shade.

Method Two - Curved Top

In order to maintain the grain line and a straight bottom edge, the top of the fabric is shaped first, then gathered onto a rod.

Measuring

Length: Finished length + double hem + seam allowance + poufs
Width: 2½ x to 3x fullness
Casing: Make a strip length of arch top + 2" by depth needed for rod casing, ruffle if used, and seam allowances.

1. Prepare fabric, seaming for width. Press and stitch 1" double side hems. Fold in half lengthwise.

2. Make a pattern of half the arch top. Divide pattern into four or more vertical sections. Cut pattern apart and pin to fabric, spacing sections to fit fabric width. Re-draw the resulting top arch, add seam allowance.

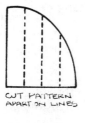

CUT PATTERN APART ON LINES

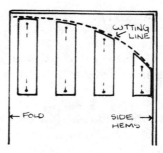

3. Make the casing (with or without ruffle). Press short ends under 1", press in half lengthwise, wrong sides together. Pin to right side of shade top. Stitch ½" seam or serge. Clip or trim seam if needed, press casing upright.

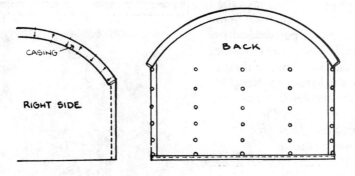

4. Mark locations for rings or shade tapes on back of shade then stitch in place.

5. Insert rod, adjust gathers evenly. Add weight bar at hem, string shade, mount and add awning cleat.

VARIATIONS

- Make a plywood frame to fit the top of the window. Staple the shade top in place to the frame.

- Use shirring or narrow smocking tape on top edge. Gather to fit plywood frame or hang from hooks.

- Staple pleats or gathers to plywood frame. Hot glue or staple on smocked or shirred heading to fit arch.

- Insert curved rod in casing, insert hooks, hang on Kir-Flex rodding.

- Form pleats as for balloon shade. Staple to frame.

VICTORIAN CLOUD

Elegance personified!! Especially effective in moire, silk, lace, or similar fabrics. This shade takes patience, but the results are stunning. Thanks to Tony Picoy of Montserrat Tapes for sharing this idea.

Constructed basically the same as the Custom Cloud with minor adjustments.

Length: 1½ x finished length
Width: 2x fullness

1. Follow steps 2 through 5 for Custom Cloud but mark ring locations as follows. Mark top of hem, then every 6", then 10" alternately to top of shade. There should be at least 2" to 3" between the top ring and heading tape.

2. To form the front tucks stitch each 6" space together. Sew rings just below tucks. (This leaves 10" spaces between rings.)

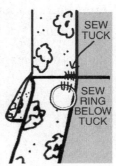

3. Continue with steps 6 through 9, tying the bottom 3 pleats into permanent poufs.

4. String and mount shade.

HEADING VARIATIONS

Shirring/Smocking Tapes

Shirring tapes and some pleating tapes have been available in this country for many years. The introduction of new lighter weight and more versatile tapes has really expanded the possibilities for easy and unusual heading details for shades.

Conso offers a delightful variety of choices for heading designs; with many specialty tapes, some of them 4" wide divided into two groups which create either double or triple fullness. There are either 3 or 4 pulling cords woven in. When applying them, keep the top stitching as close to the cord as possible so there is room along the top edge for stapling tape to mounting board without catching the fabric. Stitch beside the cords as indicated below.

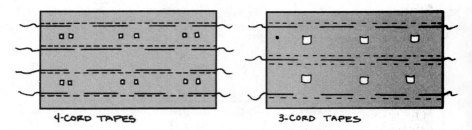

4-CORD TAPES   3-CORD TAPES

Sturdy, sheer, lightweight polyester tapes from Conso or Wrights are available in wide and narrow shirring tapes, 3 types of pleating tapes and smocking tape. They contain hook pockets and require only two lines of stitching—at top and bottom. Hook pockets should be face up, and along top edge. Stitch above top cord if hanging on hooks, below cord if stapling to mounting board.

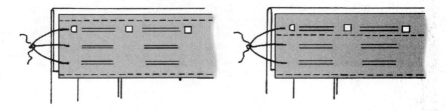

Conso and Wrights products include shirring tapes and pencil pleating tape as well as the standard Roman shade and Austrian tapes.

Gathered Headings

Gathered headings formed by casings are of two basic styles—plain or with ruffles. To determine the size of the rod casing pin your fabric around the rod or pole, mark, un-pin and measure. Take care not to pin the fabric too tight.

Variations are achieved with different types and sizes of rods:

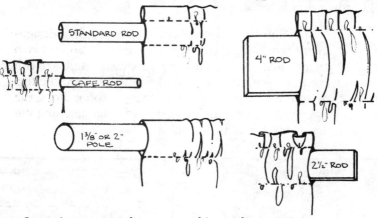

Sometimes more than one rod is used:

Some headings have both special smocking tape and rod casing.

HEM VARIATIONS

Plain

a. Rod casing at bottom edge. Lowered shade looks like illustration. When pulled, rod moves toward shade back, forming poufs.

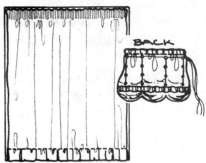

b. Weight rod can be fabric covered and tacked below ring locations, or small rods can be slipped through the rings and tacked in place.

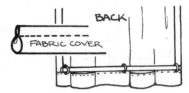

Ruffled

A ruffle can be stitched at the bottom of a cloud shade. To show below poufs when shade is raised, it must be deeper than ½ the distance between rings. The depth or number of ruffles can be changed for different effects. For ruffles the rod should be attached as in illustration 'b' above.

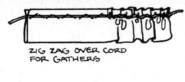

ZIG ZAG OVER CORD FOR GATHERS

STITCH TO RIGHT SIDE OF SHADE.

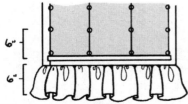

NOTE: Europeans often eliminate the weight rod in favor of drapery weights tacked at bottom ring locations, or use no weights. The result is more informal, less controlled.

MOUNTING VARIATIONS ━━━━━

Mounting Board Options (see pages 11 and 12.)

- Staple through gathers to front of board. Hide staples in folds.

- Turn back top edge of fabric, staple through shirring or smocking tape into board. Re-adjust fabric.

- Attach fabric flap which is stapled to board.

- Form box pleats and staple to top of board.

- Mount rod on front of board.

- Put velcro on front of mounting board and on top edge of shade.

Rods and Poles

A mounting board is usually installed under or behind the rod so the strain on the cords is on the board, OR screw eyes may be placed in window frame. Install shade on rod, either casing style or with drapery hooks.

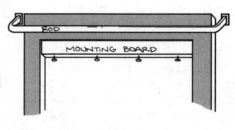

A new rod from Kirsch features Velcro hook tape applied to the front edge. With shirring and smocking tapes now being made with fuzzy loops woven in, mounting window treatments becomes easier than ever.

Chapter Eight

Balloon Shades

The balloon shade is related to both Roman and Austrian shades. It is flat and tailored when lowered, falling from inverted box pleats. It swags and poufs at the bottom when raised or when pleats are permanently tied.

Balloon shades have become a symbol of custom decorating. They can be found in many of today's decorating magazines.

Though they may be constructed in almost any fabric, softer fabrics will swag more easily and gracefully. Dressing the balloon shade requires pulling the swags out and down as they go up. After awhile they train themselves. Another trick that works well is to hold the bottom rod and swing it out to catch it full of air as you quickly pull up the shade. More than any other shade—the balloon pleats need hand shaping.

A shorter balloon shade can be constructed as a valance for use with shades, blinds, curtains or drapes. Decorators sometimes tuck tissue paper into balloon valances to help them maintain a full soft look.

Measuring

Length: a.   Finished length minus 5" for a flat shade when down
            b.   Window opening +10" or more for a poufed shade

Width: Double finished width plus 3" for side hems

Hem Skirt (see page 21):

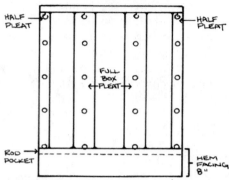

                   9½" deep x
                   finished width
                   + 2" (Cut two)

The distance between pleats on a balloon shade is usually 9" to 12". Given a free choice, I would choose 12". For example on a 36" shade there could be four pleats 9" apart, or three pleats 12" apart. Choosing 12" means less fabric width, fewer rings and cords, and less time expended. However, if a seam would fall behind a pleat if I used 9" but would not be easily concealed with 12" pleats, I would make the change.

Use a piece of fabric or paper to test and pre-determine pleat placement. Include seams if necessary (seams are best hidden inside a pleat), and pin and fold the strip to your cutting board or work surface. Illustrated: 36" shade with three equal pleats.

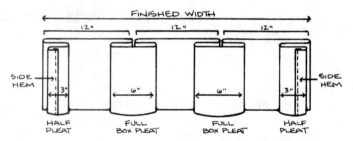

1. Prepare fabric, seaming for added width if needed. Press seams open.

2. Turn under ½" on each side edge, then 1" to form 1" side hems. Stitch or fuse hems.

3. Working on cutting board or work surface, with wrong side down, fold box-pleats as follows—one half pleat at each side hem, one full box pleat at each marked interval in the body of the shade. Press pleats then pin.

NOTE: If your fabric resists sharp creases, you may wish to stitch along the edges of the pleats on the underside ⅛" from the fold.

4. On shade back, mark ring locations in the center of the box pleats and along the side hems. (Standard method: rings 6" apart.) Stitch rings in place except for ring at hem edge. Add these rings after hem is attached. If using ring tape, stitch the tape up the center of the full box pleats and along the side hem edges according to directions in Basic Roman chapter. Place first ring ⅝" above the bottom cut edge. Re-pin pleats.

5. Follow directions on page 17 for making and attaching a separate hem.

6. String and mount following steps 7 through 10 for Standard Method.

Variations

Balloon Cloud

The Balloon Cloud on page 59 is an easy alternative to the traditional pleated balloon. It is a cloud shade in the true sense because the shade is gathered rather than pleated at the bottom, but the box pleated top is typical balloon detailing.

Contrast Pleats

Fabric of a different color or print can be used inside the box pleats. This requires lots of piecing and planning — but is a custom touch.

Ring Tape

Loop Shade Tape, regular Roman Ring Tape, or Buttoneer fasteners may be substituted for the individually sewn rings.

Bound Hem

Make shade 12" longer than finished length. Bind bottom edge with a strip of matching fabric 3" deep and finished width +2". Press ½" under on each long edge and 1" on each short edge. Pin in place over hem edge.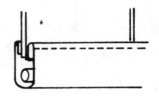
Stitch to form rod pocket. Tie bottom two pleats into permanent poufs.

Tailored Pleated Hem

Add 6" to finished length. Stitch or fuse a 2" double hem before forming pleats. Stitch 1" twill tape across back to form rod pocket 6" from bottom edge after pleats are formed. If desired, stitch pleats in hem or decorative areas. Pleats create a tailored 'skirt' when shade is raised.

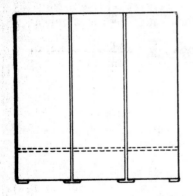
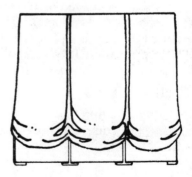

BALLOON SHADE VARIATIONS

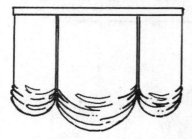

Plain skirt, cording at mounting bar, unequal pleat spacing.

Shirred or smocked heading separate strip — add after mounting.

Tailored pleats. Decorative cording added.

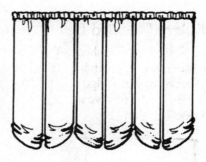

Box pleats added at center of each swag. Shirred cording at top.

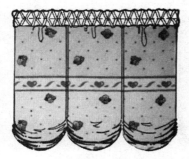

Contrast color or ribbon inside box pleats. Smocked separate heading strip.

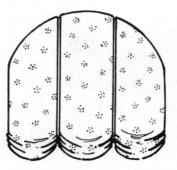

Arch top balloon. Make arch frame. Wrap and staple balloon. Cut away excess fabric.

CLOUD AND BALLOON STRINGING VARIATIONS

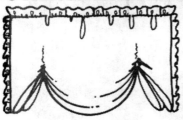

Butterfly Cloud

No cords on sides, wider spacing at center

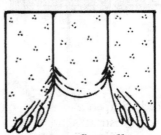

Butterfly Balloon

Equal spacing of cords, no cords on sides.

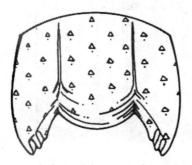

Curved top Butterfly Balloon — 2 cords.

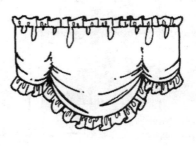

Equal tension on all four cords. Center panel 2x side panels.

No side cords. Multiple center swags.

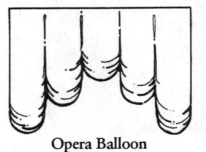

Opera Balloon

Adjust cord lengths to create 'arched' pleats.

Austrian Shades

Softly draped and gathered, Austrian shades make a formal and elegant statement at a window. If you want a plain sheer shade, my advice generally would be *buy it*. But if you want something special and out of the ordinary, it will be worth the time and effort to make it.

Some time ago I decided to make an Austrian shade from a black and white print polyester interlock knit. I was delighted with the results for a number of reasons. The fabric draped and gathered beautifully, the shade cords did not have to be released for washing, and the shade required no ironing or steaming — only a cool dryer and it was ready to hang again. Cleaning and pressing an Austrian shade is an expensive proposition. A truly easy care shade is worth some initial effort.

Austrian ring tape has woven-in shirring cords with rings spaced 12" apart.

BASIC AUSTRIAN WITH RING TAPE ▬▬

Measuring

To determine amount of fabric needed, first measure window width. Decide how many scallops you want and how wide they need to be. (Scallops should not be over 12" wide.)

Length: 2x finished length for medium weight
3x finished length for sheers

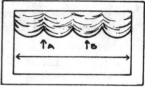

Decide if finished length is at top (a) or bottom (b) of swag. Swag hangs down about 3" longer at the bottom than where it's gathered up.

Width: Measure width of window   ____
Multiply no of swags x 3" or 4"   ____
Add 3" for side seams   ____
Total Width (approx 1⅓ fullness)   ____

Be sure to allow extra if fabric width must be seamed.

1. Sew fabric panels together. Use French seams or serger on sheer fabrics. See page 60. Press 1½" single hems on sides and double 1½" seam at bottom Stitch the bottom hem. Zig zag, hem or bind top edge of shade.

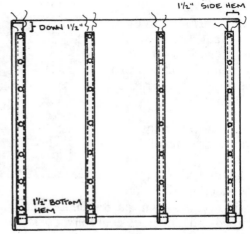

2. Cut lengths of Austrian ring tape finished length minus 2", making the first cut 1" below a ring.. Knot the ends of the shirring cords so they cannot pull out.

3. Pin tapes 1½" down from top of shade and covering side hems. Stitch from bottom to top on both sides of tapes. Turn up the extra 1" at bottom and sew into loops for weight bar.

NOTE: Stitching need not be perfect, it disappears into the gathers.

4. Since you have allowed up to 4" extra for each swag, the shade will be wider at the top than the window. Pin tucks at top on each side of the tapes as shown, until shade fits mounting board.

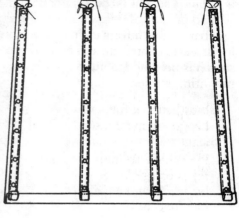

5. A weight bar at the hem is needed to help the shade operate smoothly. To hold the weight rod securely in the loops at the bottom of the shade, encase the rod in fabric or ribbon tubing.

6. Pull the two knotted cords in each tape to gather the shade to the desired length. Knot the cords to prevent gathers from slipping. **Do not cut the cords** so they can be released for cleaning if desired. Make sure all rings are still even across the shade after gathering.

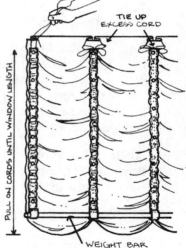

TIE UP EXCESS CORD

PULL ON CORDS UNTIL WINDOW LENGTH

WEIGHT BAR

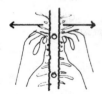

To help even out the gathers it helps to grasp them on each side of the ring tape and give a firm tug.

7. To mount and string the shade follow directions for Standard Roman Shade.

FULL AUSTRIAN

Triple length for a rich look. A decorated shirred strip has been added after mounting shade.

Width: 1½ x fullness
Length: Triple finished length

Plan shade so loop tapes or ring tapes fall on seams and equally in between.

1. Prepare fabric, press 1½" single side hems. Press and stitch double 1½" bottom hem.

2. Cut Australian Loop tapes the cut length minus 1½". Make first cut 1½" below a loop. Mark tapes 1½" from bottom cut then about every 30". Pin tapes to shade, leaving the 1½" extension which will become the rod loop. Tapes will be approximately 18" apart

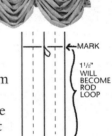

3. Stitch each side of tape, bottom to top, backtacking at top of hem. Zig zag or bind the top edge of shade. Do not catch pulling cords in stitches.

4. Lay shade flat and anchor bottom edge.

5. Lift out shirring cords at top of shade. Pull cords with one hand as you push with the other. Using marked rings or loops as guides for keeping gathers even, work in small sections from tape to tape until shade is desired length. Securely knot shirring cords.

6. Fold tape extensions into loops to hold fabric-covered weight bar. Adjust gathers and tack tapes to rod.

7. Pin small tucks on either side of tapes at shade top, until shade fits mounting board.

8. Mount and string shade as for Standard Roman. Make a decorative shirring or smocking strip and attach to top of shade with staples.

DELUXE AUSTRIAN

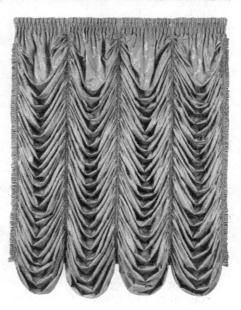

This is a full and very luxurious shade. The heading can be a shirring or smocking tape, stitched into the shade top as illustrated.

> Width: Double
> Length: Triple finished length

Follow instructions for Full Austrian except add smocking tape heading. See Custom Cloud page 56.

Plan shade so ring tapes fall on seams and equally in between.

RINGLESS AUSTRIAN

This simple and attractive method uses European 2-cord transparent shirring tape. This sturdy, sheer tape has frequent built-in cross-thread cord sites through which the pulling cord is threaded. This eliminates the need for rings. These directions produce a Basic Austrian, but the 2-cord tape may be used for any of the methods shown.

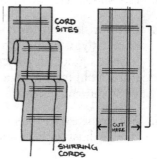

1. Follow Basic Austrian method for measuring and preparing fabric. Press single 1" side hems. Press and stitch double 1½" bottom hem.

2. Cut tapes same as cut length of shade minus 1½". Mark bottom cord site and make first cut 3" below site, then measure and cut tape. Using a fabric marker or other marker, mark every 12" from bottom cord site. These guidelines help in lining up gathers.

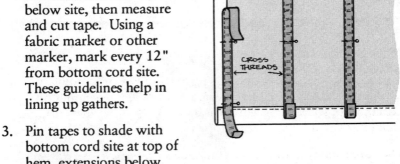

3. Pin tapes to shade with bottom cord site at top of hem, extensions below, and side tapes covering hem edges. Stitch each side of tape from bottom to top, backstitching at top of hem. Knot bottom cords.

4. Fold extensions into loops to hold weight bar. Stitch securely with small stitches through hem stitches.

5. Lift out top ends of shirring cords. Pull cords as you push in gathers with other hand. Work in small sections from tape to tape, until shade is desired length and guide marks are even. Securely knot pulling cords. Bundle excess above knot, or cut off if you don't need to flatten shade for washing or cleaning.

6. Thread tapestry needle with fine cord. Thread through cord sites. Space 6" or more depending on fabric and look desired. Anchor cords securely at top of hem. Add dab of glue or seam sealant to knots.

   NOTE: A cord site will appear at the top of every other gather.

cord sites

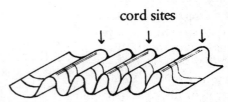

7. String and mount shade following directions for Standard Roman shade.

Chapter Ten

Shade Toppers

If you prefer the layered look at your windows, try adding a shade topper, such as a valance, swag, or cornice. Depending on your decorating style, mini blinds, pleated blinds, verticals, curtains, and draperies can all benefit from one of these additions.

They are usually about ⅛ the length of a drapery, ⅓ the length of a shade treatment, 4" wider and 2" deeper than the treatment beneath—governed by the size and type of rod and treatment to be covered and the amount of clearance needed. Toppers may be mounted on rods or stapled to mounting boards.

Basic Rod Types	
Standard Oval Curtain Rod	4½" Continental® or Dauphine®
2½" Continental® or Dauphine®	1⅜" or 2" Wood or Metal Rod
Round cafe rod	Combinations of rods

Pin fabric around rod to determine size of casing needed

Shirring, smocking, pleating and ring tapes make window toppers quick and easy. Ornate headings are as easy as stitching a few straight lines and pulling the cords! Tapes are available for double or triple fullness. Some tapes feature woven-in hook pockets for the option of hanging the topper on hooks (as opposed to stapling to a mounting board).

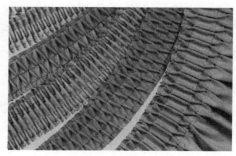

Double Fullness

If using hooks, be sure hook pockets are up when stitching tapes in place. Otherwise, stitch as close as possible to the cord, allowing room along the top edge of the tape for stapling it to the mounting board.

Triple Fullness

VALANCES

GATHERED VALANCE

The simplest and most common. A length of fabric (double to triple fullness) with a plain or ruffled casing on top, and a double 1" or 2" bottom hem is gathered onto a rod.

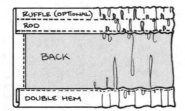

NOTE: When this basic valance is made longer, and rings or shade tapes are added, it becomes a cloud valance.

GATHERED DOUBLE ROD VALANCE

Double to triple width fabric is gathered onto two rods, with either plain casings or headings and ruffles.

Two standard rods can be spaced to give the appearance of using the more expensive 4½" Continental® or Dauphine® rod.

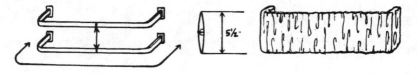

Valance may be a single layer with casings and hems, or a 'sleeve' with casing lines.

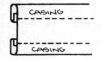 

Many variations are possible by changing the width and number of rods, the spacing, and the use of plain casings or ruffled headings.

CLOUD VALANCE — Casing Top

Really just a short cloud shade, this is a flat piece of fabric which gets its shape by tying rings into swag poufs and gathering the top. See Cloud Shade chapter for details on rods and headings.

Depth: Finished length + headings, hems, poufs
Width: Double to triple fullness

1. Cut and seam fabric for width. Plan seams to fall behind row of rings. Make double 1" side and bottom hems.

2. Turn and press ½" at top edge, then amount for casing and ruffle.

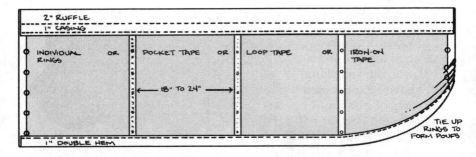

3. Sew a row of rings, or strip of shade tape with first ring at top of hem, at each side hem and at intervals of 18" to 24" depending on number of swag poufs needed.

4. Tie up bottom three or four rings of each row to create the permanent poufs. You can adjust length of valance by how many and how tightly you tie the rings.

5. Add weight rod (optional), and mount at window. Adjust gathers.

CLOUD VALANCE — Ruffle Hem

The ruffle is sewn to the straight hem edge. It will swag when cords are tied. Make ruffle 2x finished depth + 1" for seam allowance, and 2x finished length. See page 73.

1. Press short ends to wrong side then fold in half lengthwise.

2. Zig zag over cord and pull to gather or use ruffler or shirring foot.

3. Pin ruffle to right side of valance and stitch ½" seam, then zig zag raw edge. OR serge ruffle to valance. Press.

4. Attach fabric covered weight bar by tacking at ring locations. Mount valance at window.

SMOCKED CLOUD VALANCE

Constructed the same as for a casing top valance, but smocking or shirring tape is used in place of a casing. See pages 57-59.

SMOCKED DOUBLE ROD VALANCE

This valance features a row of smocking tape across the center and makes a self-lined valance 15" deep.

1. Cut and seam valance fabric 31" long and 2½x fullness. Press 1" side hems.

2. Fold top edge down and bottom edge up 8", overlapping 1" in the middle. Press.

3. Pin a row of 2" smocking tape down the center on the wrong side. Fold ends of tape under 1½", pull out pulling cords, stitch tape along top and bottom edge.

4. Stitch 2" from top; repeat at bottom to form rod casing.

5. Knot cords at each end, pull up tapes pushing fabric snugly, then ease out to fit rods. Adjust with fingers.

6. Insert rods and mount. Arrange fabric fullness evenly along top and bottom rods.

SMOCKED SLEEVE VALANCES

These terrific smocked toppers fit popular 4½" Continental® and Dauphine® rods. Each valance begins as a flat rectangle of double or triple width, depending on the 4" tape of choice. After tape is applied, the fabric is sewn into a sleeve.

Simple Sleeve

This delight-
ful heading
makes a real
decorative statement.

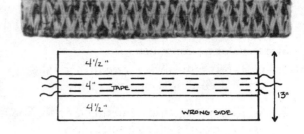

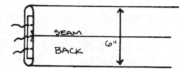

Welted Sleeve

Smocking and
welting combine for
a special look. For
another version,
leave the 2½" welt
pockets uncorded as
ruffles.

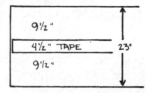

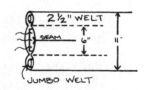

Flounce Sleeve

A soft valance
with classic lines.

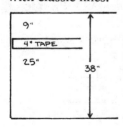

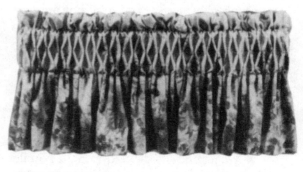

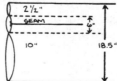

NOTE: For another look the flounce may be opened up to create a pouf effect. Stuff with tissue or cleaner bags if desired.

Sleeve Valance Construction:

1. Cut and seam fabric for width according to tape fullness and for depth according to type of valance.

2. Stitch tape to fabric, centering tape for Simple or Welted Sleeve, and 9" from top for Flounce Sleeve.

3. Fold fabric right sides together, sew ½" seam to form the sleeve.

4. Turn right side out and press ¾" side hems. Center seam behind 4" tape and press. For Welted and Flounce Sleeve stitch casings as illustrated on previous page.

5. Lift out pulling cords, knot ends. Securely anchor one end of cords. With both hands, start shirring top. Pinch and pull until smocking design is even. Bundle cords and tuck inside open end of tape or knot and cut off excess.

6. For Welted Sleeve insert 1" welting into casings. Insert dowel with nail on end through casing, tie welting to nail and pull through.

EASY POUF VALANCE

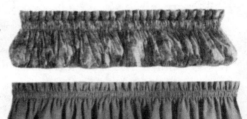

Delightfully simple to make—it adapts to all types of treatments and fabrics. Example shown with 2" ruffle.

Depth: 2x finished
   length + 1"
Width: Double to triple

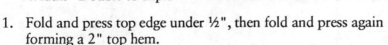

1. Fold and press top edge under ½", then fold and press again forming a 2" top hem.

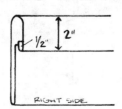

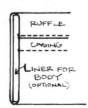

2. Bring bottom edge up and tuck ½" under top hem, pin. Stitch 2" down from fold and again 3" down to form rod pocket.

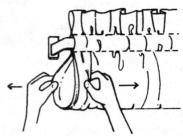

3. Slip onto rod, hand dress the poufs into controlled swags.

CUSTOM TIP: Tuck tissue paper or cleaner bags into the valance for added body and pouf. Or you may add body by inserting a strip of lining between the layers before stitching hem and casing.

POUF VALANCE WITH FLOUNCE

This easy one-piece self-lined valance forms its own ruffle at the hem. Just 4 rows of stitching! Example makes a 15" valance of 2½" fullness.

1. Prepare fabric 35" deep by 2½x fullness, make 1½" side hems.

2. Press top edge down 10" and bottom edge up 5½" Stitch 1½" from top and again 3" from top to form rod pocket and ruffle.

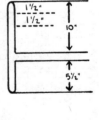

3. Overlap the raw edges by ½" and pin the excess fabric out of the way near the casings. Pin shirring tape, centered over the overlapping edges. Stitch top and bottom edges of shirring tape.

4. Shirr the fabric to finished width. Knot cord ends. Adjust gathers. Insert rod. Hand dress gathers to create swags or soft even poufs.

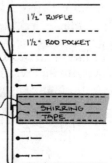

TWIST TOPPER

Just twist header round and round the rod. For a change — untwist them or mount on 1, 2 or 3 rods. Make strip 2x fullness or more. More fullness means more fabric to twist. Illustration shows 3" casing with 4" ruffles.

Same style — no twist

1. Prepare 2 fabric strips — matching or contrasting.

2. Press under ³/₄" on each short end; fuse. Pin strips right sides together and stitch each long edge in a ¹/₂" seam. Turn and press. Or pin strips *wrong* sides together and decoratively serge or bind the long edges together.

3. Stitch a 3" casing down the center of the strip. Insert 2½" rod, gather and twist the casing round and round on the rod.

Variations

*   Experiment with different size rods and ruffles.
*   Adjust ruffles in uneven twists, for example 6" of straight gathers then a twist, etc.
*   Same fabric on both sides, colored binding or serging on edges.

EASY PINCH PLEAT VALANCE

Ideally a pleat should fall on the outer corners of the valance. When determining width of rod or mounting board, pleat the tape, then measure to determine board length, and side returns.

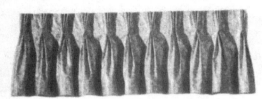

1. Prepare valance strip 2½x fullness and desired depth plus 2" double hem and 2" top turn down. Make 1" double side hems, 2" bottom hem. Press top edge down 2".

2. Turn under 1½" on each end of tape, knot cords. Pin tape to valance ½" down from top edge, hook pockets up. Stitch tape. Hold cords at one side and push first

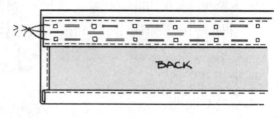

set of pleats into position. Go to next set and push; continue across valance. Tie cords into bundles and slip under open end of tape or wrap on floss holder.

3. Hang on hooks, or staple to mounting board.

CORNICES

These firm box-like frames are usually padded and made of wood. Fabric can also be smocked, shirred, corded. There are many ways to make a cornice — here are some that are easy and inexpensive.

STIFFENED BUCKRAM ON A ROD

Stiffened buckram such as Conso's Permette is flexible yet sturdy. Available in 11" and 36" depth. Washable and cleanable.

1. Cut strip desired width plus returns. Use the 11" depth, or splice by overlapping, stitching or gluing.

2. Stitch a 2" strip of lining ½" from the top and side edges to form rod casing.

3. Wrap polyester fleece around buckram. Stitch, taking care not to stitch rod pocket closed.

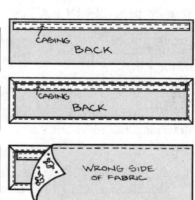

4. Cut fabric 3" longer and 2" wider than buckram. Place fabric right side on buckram wrong side, matching top edges. Stitch a ½" seam.

5. Flip fabric to right side. Turn in side and bottom edges and stitch by hand. Insert rod and mount.

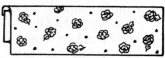

MOUNTING BOARD

A board fastened above the window with angle irons creates a base on which

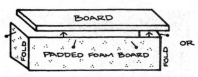

many types of treatments can be mounted. The board must be wide enough and long enough to clear the window treatment below.

Cut, score, and fold a length of cardboard or foam board to fit front and sides of mounting board. Pad and cover with fabric. Tack it to outer edges of board, or leave fabric "flange" to staple to top of board (or use iron-on loop tape on cornice, hook tape on board).

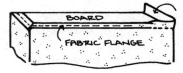

SCORED CARDBOARD

In place of using a mounting board, a cornice can be made entirely of cardboard. Cut a sturdy piece to size as shown, then score and bend it to form the cornice. Tape sides together, then cover with padding and fabric. Attach to window frame with ordinary straight pins or use a hammer to drive in pushpins. For frameless windows, attach a small block of wood to the wall first, then glue or tack the cornice to the wood block. Or set the cornice on a curtain rod as shown in illustration.

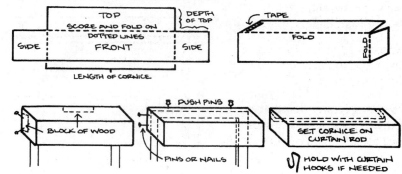

DOUBLE ROD 'CORNICE'

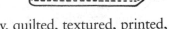

The tailored appearance belies the fact that it is technically a valance.

Good fabric choices are medium-heavy, quilted, textured, printed, horizontally striped, or banded.

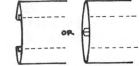

Width: Front of rod + returns, side hems
Depth: Finished length + casings, hems

1. Pin fabric around rod to determine depth of casings. Add ½" for each hem. Prepare fabric strip, seaming if necessary for width.

2. Make casings at top and bottom (or use sleeve technique). Insert rods, and mount.

PANEL SWAGS

These simple toppers are rectangles of fabric with rod casings on each end.

Width: 2x (to 3x) fullness of rod area to be covered
Length: Drape measuring tape from rod. Add for casings (and ruffle).

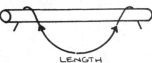

LENGTH

Method One

1. Sew 1" double hems on top and bottom edges.

2. Fold ends under ½" on each side edge, then press under for casing (and ruffle). Stitch hem edge, stitch again for ruffle.

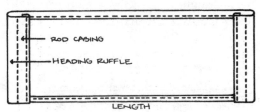

ROD CASING
HEADING RUFFLE
LENGTH

Method Two — Lined or Reversible Swags.

1. Place wrong sides together. Stitch around outside edges leaving openings for rod and about 6" for turning swag.

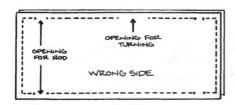
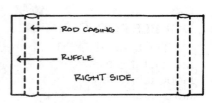

2. Turn right side out, stitch casing lines, close 6" opening.

Styling Swags — Lay swags on a table and try out different configurations.

CROSSOVER TWISTS

SIDE BY SIDE TWISTS

REVERSE TWISTS

SIDE BY SIDE TWISTS

REVERSE TWISTS

Method Three — Shaped Swags

This method of shaping gives the swag a more controlled drape.

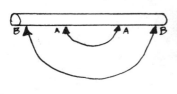

Cut swag as illustrated. Prepare casing to fit rod. Slip over ends and stitch.

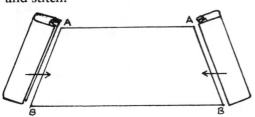
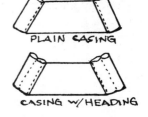
PLAIN CASING

CASING W/ HEADING

SIDE BY SIDE

CROSS OVER

EASY DRAPED SWAGS ▬▬▬▬

A length of fabric, lined or unlined, is draped across or around a rod, through swag holders, rings, or other devices. For some people, controlling the gathers and fullness is important, for others the charm of this technique is that what you get is 'one of a kind.' Whatever you choose—these are exciting and fun to create.

WINDOW SCARF

Mount swag holders at corners of window. Measure the length of the sides (jabots) and width of window area to be covered. Fabric can go part way down the sides or all the way to the floor and even be 'puddled' for effect.

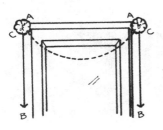

A - A = window width; top of swag
C - C = bottom edge of swag
A - B = jabot length (side panel)

1. Prepare fabric length, hem ends and sides. Using pins, center and mark the window width (A - A) on one long edge. Measure and mark 6" out from window width on opposite side.

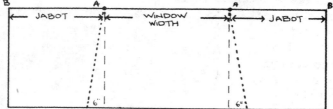

2. Gather fabric into fan fold pleats along the dotted lines. Holding pleats in place (or tie them loosely) place them on swag holders and adjust pleats.

'COMBO' SWAG

This treatment combines angled jabots into one piece of fabric.

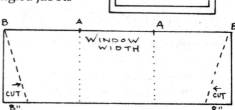

1. Measure window as for window scarf above. Cut fabric length and mark window width.

On opposite long edge measure in 8" from each end. Cut to opposite corner. Repeat for lining.

2. Sew ½" seam allowance leaving opening for turning. Trim corners, turn right side out. Press. Close opening.

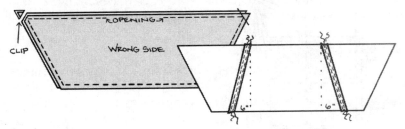

3. Mark window width on long edge. Mark 6" wider than window width on opposite (short) edge. Gather fabric into soft folds on an angle along this line, or stitch shirring tape along the angle and pull up.

4. Place on swag holders (A). Arrange folds for desired effect. Fan folds will give a more controlled jabot. Shirring is more informal, as pleats will flare a little more.

NOTE: Some designers reverse the swag when placing it on the brackets causing the pleats to fall to the outside (B).

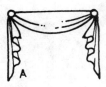
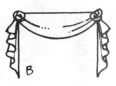

Hardware choices for swag treatments abound. Swag and rosette brackets come in spiral, square, heart and tulip shapes. One of the most extensive lines available is from Claesson. Their holders can also accommodate multiple swags. Infinity Rings are designed to be portable, they can be hung on cup hooks. In addition consider using drapery holdbacks, small grapevine wreaths, towel rings, wood or metal rings—whatever works.

FREE FORM SWAGS

Some people call these playful treatments "loops and swoops"—an apt description. There is no right or wrong. Yards of fabric are draped, swagged, puddled. To get an idea of the length you need use ribbon, yarn or cord. Drape it and tape it to the pole or brackets.

When you begin to work with the fabric itself, you may use pins, tacks (for wood poles) tape, Velcro dots or other devices to help hold the fabric in position. Experimenting is half the fun. Enjoy!

Chapter Eleven

Roller Shades

You can make your own roller shades in a variety of ways. The construction cost will vary with different methods as will the appearance—mainly from the street side. Nonbacked single-layer shades show color to the exterior, while backed methods are more opaque and allow no light or color at all if constructed from a black-out or room-darkening backing. Choosing your preferred method will depend in part on whether you don't mind various window treatment colors on the exterior or you prefer a more uniform exterior look on all windows.

With construction affecting finished product, it is advisable to make a test sample of methods you are considering. This will allow you to determine if the weight of face fabric and backing are compatible so the shade will roll smoothly.

ANATOMY OF A SHADE

The roller is quite simple and has changed very little since it was invented in 1864 by Stewart Hartshorn. A spring set into the roller catches a notched wheel as the shade is adjusted at the window.

Rollers come in three types — wood, cardboard (convolute), and steel. You can staple shades to wood or cardboard (use only ¼" or ³⁄₁₆" staples), or use tape on all types.

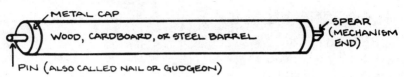

Window width is related to roller diameter. As a window gets wider, the diameter of the roller increases to assure strength and resistance to sagging. Roller diameter varies from ¹⁵⁄₁₆" for 37" to 1¼" for 80" rollers in wood and cardboard. Steel rollers range from 1" for 37" shades to 3" for 7' to 15' shades.

If your shade will be heavier than average, as for a laminated shade, it will be best to select a heavy duty roller. A very long shade will also require a heavy duty roller. The added expense is slight; the benefits well worth the cost.

Always shorten a roller from pin end to avoid disturbing the roller spring mechanism.

Remove the pin with pliers, and pull off the metal cap. Saw roller to size,

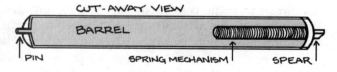

replace the cap, and hammer the pin into place. Be sure the pin goes in straight.

You will want to be familiar with the three widths illustrated below. Keep in mind that for installation purposes **rollers are always measured from tip-to-tip.**

Bare rollers can be purchased cut-to-fit from shade shops and often in hardware or variety and some mail order

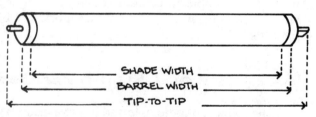

stores. If necessary, you can purchase an inexpensive ready-made shade, remove the plastic and use its roller and slat. The basic danger of this is that the inexpensive roller may not have a spring strong enough to lift the weight of a laminated fabric shade. If you do choose this method, recycle the plastic shade by using it for a pattern, then as a drop cloth for painting or arts and crafts projects.

MOUNTING METHODS

Roller shades are mounted in one of two ways — reverse roll or conventional roll. In either case it is the same roller. It is just a matter of positioning the spear and the way the shade is mounted on the roller that makes the difference.

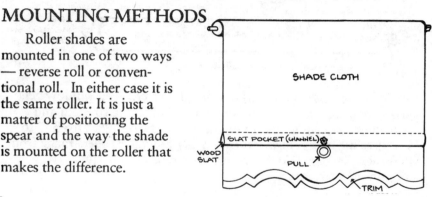

Reverse Roll

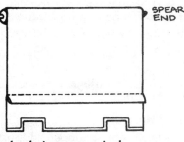

The spear (flat) end should be on your right when the fabric side of the shade faces you. The shade cloth is in front of the roller causing the shade to sit out from the window a bit. This method avoids handles or projections, the roller does not show, but streaks of light are more likely along the edges of the shade in some window types.

Conventional Roll

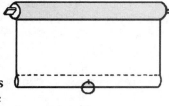

The spear is on your left. The shade fabric comes off the back of the shade causing the shade to fit closer to the window. This prevents light streaks and saves energy. The roller will show unless a cornice or valance is used.

The Wooden Slat

The wooden slat across the bottom of a shade is not necessary, but helps the shade hold its shape and prevents curling. Slats need about a 1¼" tuck which can be on the front or back side of the shade. The channel or tuck should be at least 2" above the top of the decorative edge, if one is used.

INSTALLING BRACKETS & ROLLERS

It is most common to install the brackets first, then cut the roller, place in the brackets and check for fit. Accurate measurements are extremely important. An inaccuracy of even ¼" can prevent smooth action and fit. Cloth tape measures or strings can stretch, so use a wood rule or metal tape. Make sure brackets are level or the shade may not roll properly.

Windows may look the same size, but seldom are. Frames often vary slightly from top to bottom and from one window to another. For this reason be sure to mark each roller so it will be placed in the correct window.

There are many styles of brackets for different purposes and window types. (See Directory of Shade Brackets page 124.) In addition there are heavy duty and extension brackets in most styles to accommodate long, heavy, or thick shades. The longer a shade is, or the more textured the fabric is, the 'fatter' it gets on the roller. This may require the use of heavy duty or extension brackets to allow for the extra weight and space. It will usually also call for the heavy duty roller mentioned earlier. Four to five feet in length is about maximum in a laminated shade for a regular roller.

Inside Brackets

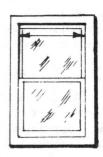

Measure from one inside surface of the window frame to the opposite inside surface. If your roller is being cut for you, indicate this is tip-to-tip measurement for an IBM (inside bracket mount); thus the dealer will automatically subtract a scant ⅛" for clearance in the window. If brackets are already mounted and you are cutting your own roller, be sure you measure "surface to surface" and subtract ⅛" to obtain the proper tip-to-tip measurement. To allow the shade ample room to roll without binding fasten brackets at least 1¼" from the top of the window.

NOTE: Since the actual diameter of roller plus shade will not be known until the shade is completed, you may wish to mark bracket positions and wait to install them until the shade is finished.

Outside Brackets

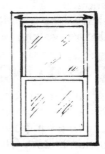

Mount the brackets on trim or wall. Position brackets so there will be 1½" to 2" of overlap on the window frame. This helps prevent light streaks along the sides of the shade.

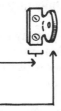

Bracket Foot - this is mounting plate, NOT bracket measuring point.

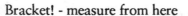

Bracket! - measure from here

Ceiling Brackets

It is recommended that the shade overlap the window frame 1½" to 2". For length measure from the ceiling to the window sill.

Bottom-Up Installation

Directions are same as for inside or outside mount, but the brackets are installed at the bottom of the window. Brackets may be installed on sill or floor.

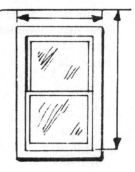

Shade Preparations

Choose Shade Fabric

Firmly woven fabric is important, especially for larger shades. Looser weaves will tend to stretch and ravel. Fabric may be placed on the crosswise direction, design permitting, since it will be stabilized when fused, bonded, or glued. This will allow wider shades than normal fabric width of 45" or 54", with no splices. It is a helpful for short but wide ranch style windows.

Make a Test Sample

Select the methods you feel are best for your fabric and the location of the shade. Evaluate them and make a selection.

The following questions may help you make a decision:

- Is the method compatible with the fabric to produce enough but not too much body? If the backing is too light, the shade edges ripple and the shade may not have enough body to maintain its shape. Liquid stiffeners often don't work on fabrics treated with stain-resistant finishes.

- Is room darkening desired? Commercial blackout backings can provide complete darkening. Some methods are more translucent than others. Hold samples up to light.

- What about sun fading? Some fading can be expected over a period of time. Bright and dark colors are most susceptible. Laminated shades are most protected. Light colors fade least.

- How much am I willing or able to spend? No matter what method you choose, you will be saving 40% to 60% (or more) over a custom shade.

- What is available in my area? Not all backings or stiffeners are readily available, so having a variety of choices is an advantage. Fusible webs and drapery linings are found in most fabric shops and can often be mail ordered. Commercial backings are available from shade shops and sometimes by mail. Stiffeners and sprays are usually found in fabric stores, drapery or shade shops, and by mail.

Assemble Materials

Roller	Scissors
Brackets	Press Cloth
Fabric	Backing or stiffener
Slat	Staple gun or tape
Shade Pull	Carpenter's square
Trim	Cardboard cutting board
Rulers	Straight Edge Guides
Iron	Glue or Fray Check™

Work Surface

A surface large enough to support the entire shade is most desirable. A shade hanging over the edge of an ironing board or table can easily be stretched or distorted. Accurate measurements may be affected.

Cutting to General Size

Cut sharp clean edges with no raveling. Strings or ravelings that get between the fabric and backing during the bonding process will show through as dark lines in a translucent shade.

If your fabric requires splicing, you will be preparing the cut edges of the splices at this time, too. (See Splicing Pointers page 116.)

Take your time as you lay out your fabric. Be sure you have design motifs centered where they look their best. Pay special attention to stripes and one way designs. Care now pays dividends later.

Width

Cut the fabric (and backing if one is used) one to two inches wider — approximately the tip-to-tip measurement of the roller.

Length

Measure area shade is to cover and add 12" to 16" for roll-over. This is the safety margin left on the roller. It prevents the shade from being torn from the roller when the shade is pulled. Twelve inches is standard roll-over; sixteen if the hem is cut into a deep ornamental shape.

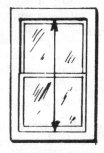

CONSTRUCTION METHODS ▬▬▬

FUSIBLE BACKINGS

Two fusible backings with different characteristics are widely available. Pellon's Wonder Shade® is a 36" wide room darkening or black out type, which appears white from the outside. HTC's Fuse-A-Shade® is translucent and allows some light to enter through the shade and may exhibit some "show through" of design when lighted from the inside at night. It is available by the yard in 45" and 60" (harder to find) widths, and in kits which contain a length of backing, a cardboard ratchet style roller, a plastic hem bar, and brackets.

When purchasing yardage, ask to have the backing rolled rather than folded. Even though the folds will probably press out in the bonding process, it will be easier to handle and to splice if it is kept smooth.

These backings are not recommended for sheer or very lightweight fabrics. Medium weight firmly woven fabrics will give good results. Occasionally when heavier fabrics are bonded they roll well in conventional roll, but pucker if reverse rolled. It is advisable to test roll your sample. If puckering is a problem, you may need to use a conventional roll installation and conceal the roller with a cornice or valance.

Illustration A shows the most common shade layout with the lengthwise grain running vertically on the shade.

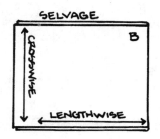

For splices or to improve the roll of the shade (conventional or reverse), Illustration B shows how the grain can be run horizontally across the shade.

Because fabric weight and texture may affect fusing time, it is advisable to make a 9" or 10" square test sample. With iron at wool/steam setting determine the time needed for a secure bond. Lighter weight fabrics may fuse quickly by simply gliding the iron. Others may take 5 to 15 seconds. For more steam have a spray bottle handy. If fabric bubbles, lower temperature and use a shorter pressing time.

Note: Some fabrics may not adhere to Wonder Shade®.

Your sample can also be used to test for rolling. Mark the grain-line on sample pieces before fusing. You may also test cutting techniques. A sharp utility knife, rotary cutter or scissors are all possibilities and can give you practice cutting a smooth straight line.

To avoid stretching, ridges and wrinkling it is best to work on a large padded surface rather than an ironing board. However, if you must use an ironing board, place a table adjacent so the fused portion stays flat till cool.

WONDER SHADE® ROOM DARKENING SHADE BACKING

Position Wonder Shade with fusible side up. Place decorator fabric on fusible and smooth it in place. Set iron at pre-determined setting and work from center outward. Lift and lower iron one row at a time, being careful to overlap iron prints. Smooth row with iron then go on to the next. Let shade cool completely. If any bubbles appear, prick fashion fabric with a pushpin and press.

If a splice is necessary in the backing, it is preferable to position it horizontally. Fuse the lower (hem edge) portion of the shade first. Let cool. Turn shade over; align additional length of Wonder Shade® fusible side down barely overlapping edges. Press along pieced edges using a dry sheer press cloth. Let cool. Then turn shade and finish fusing from the fabric side.

FUSE-A-SHADE® TRANSLUCENT BACKING

Begin with a test sample as described above.

Place backing on padded work surface with fusible side up. Position fabric carefully on top. Use 'wool' steam setting and a damp press cloth. Start in the center and work out to the sides, one row at a time. Press for 10-15 seconds over entire area. Use an up and down pressing motion, do not slide the iron. Let shade cool to room temperature then turn over and repeat on back side.

If the backing must be spliced, place fabric on work surface first, then position the backing pieces on top, butting or barely overlapping the smooth cut edges. Use a see-thru press cloth so you can see that your splice is accurate.

GLUING TO A SHADE BACKING

This technique, used by custom shade makers, is really quite easy and produces one of the most professional results. Heavy vinyl shades can be an aid to energy efficiency when carefully fitted to the window.

A large smooth work surface is most desirable, although it is possible to work on the floor. Be sure to cover the area with plastic if it is not washable.

The laminating glue is rolled evenly onto the shade with a short nap paint roller. The decorator fabric is then rolled and smoothed into place. Once the gluing is completed the shade is lightly ironed and allowed to dry.

Edges are trimmed and treated for ravel resistance. Decorative trim and shade pull may also be added.

There are several approaches for this method:

1. Purchase backing by the yard from a shade shop then measure, cut and laminate it yourself.

2. If you already have a good quality vinyl or cloth shade, you can laminate your fabric to it.

3. Purchase a good quality plain shade and glue the fabric to it.

If the shade has the slat at the bottom edge, you may use it that way. For custom hem if the shade is long enough, cut the slat off, move the slat tuck higher on the shade. Leave room for a decorative edge. (See Shade Trim Ideas.)

If you purchase your plain shade through a shade shop, you might have them sew the tuck where you want it and leave a plain bottom edge, You can then cut your own design and glue trim to the edge to complete the shade.

HEM DEPTH DETERMINED BY CHOICE OF HEM DESIGN

The best results will be obtained with a medium to heavy vinyl coated shade cloth. While it is possible to glue to a very inexpensive plastic shade, you will nearly always get puckers on the back side.

If possible, use a commercial laminating glue (such as Graber Laminating Adhesive or Lamashade) available in quart or gallon sizes through shade shops or drapery departments. These glues dry clear and FLEXIBLE. If you cannot locate a commercial glue, a white craft glue will work. Test it first by pouring a small amount on a piece of fabric. If it dries clear and flexible, it is a possibility. Then make a sample with fabric and shade backing, or high up on your roller shade. I have used different white glues with success, but Elmer's is unacceptable as it dries hard and too stiff.

BONDING WITH LAMINATING OR CRAFT GLUE

1. Cover the unpadded work surface with brown paper or heavy plastic. Masking tape all the edges of the backing which has been pre-cut to general size (see page 108), fastening one edge along the edge of the table. This serves as a guideline for a straight edge.

2. Center the fabric over the backing, then tape the top edge in place about 1" above the backing. (If you are working on a ready-made shade, tape the fabric just below the roller.)

3. Now carefully roll the fabric onto a tube, keeping the edge along the table straight and even. To start bring the fabric back over the tube until side edges line up. Then roll all the way to the masking tape.

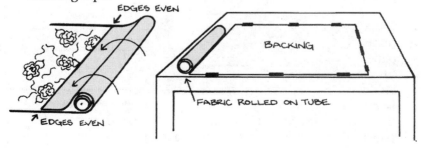

4. Pour glue into a paint roller pan, then thoroughly coat a short nap or sponge roller. Now roll quickly and evenly until a thin coat of glue covers the entire backing. There must be no skips or dry areas. If the glue is applied too thick, it may soak through to the front when fabric is applied.

5. Begin to roll the fabric slowly and evenly onto the wet glue, smoothing with your hands as you go. (Always work WITH stripes, not across them.) Then take a medium warm iron and go over the whole shade, slowly and evenly. This helps to start the glue drying and removes air pockets, assuring a good bond. Allow the glue to dry overnight if possible (at least 8 hours) before cutting and shaping

Clean up glue with water immediately after finishing. Glue is water soluble while wet, but permanent when dry. Wear old clothes. If you need to carry over the gluing to another day, wrap the paint roller in plastic and put it in the refrigerator. It will keep for well over a week this way.

NOTE: Be sure to read Splicing Pointers for face fabric details.

A FUSIBLE 'SANDWICH' — Fabric/Fusible/Backing
This method uses the heat sensitive webbings described in Time Savers. It produces a durable and very attractive shade though it takes more time and patience to construct, but the shades always roll well in conventional or reverse. Materials are readily available in fabric stores. Roc Lon 54" blackout lining is a popular backing.

You may also find that working with paper-backed fusible web is easier than "steam basting" or pinning standard fusible web strips.

1. Make a 'sandwich' of the face fabric and fabric backing with the fusible web in the middle. The web will need to be overlapped to create enough width, as it is only 18" wide. Be sure there are no gaps between webbing strips, OR

Use a release paper fusible and dry iron it to

the wrong side of the shade fabric. After it cools, remove the paper. Place shade fabric and backing together with fusible in the middle. Heat'n Bond's maker claims 'three times the bond of any other iron on adhesive' (good choice for heavier decorator and drapery fabrics.) Steam-A-Seam is another good choice.

2. Follow the manufacturer's directions for applying the webbing.

3. Start in the center and press your way out to the sides. Be careful not to lift or pull the fabric while it is warm or push the iron (ironing motion) hard on the fabric. This can stretch edges and cause distortion that may prevent the shade from looking attractive and hanging correctly. Be sure to steam press from both sides, allowing the fabric to cool before turning it over.

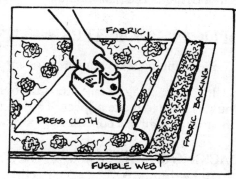

LIQUID STIFFENERS

A single layer of stiffened fabric can be used as a roller shade. With no backing, the shade will be "thinner" when rolled up, making a longer shade possible. Just be aware that the fabric color will show to the exterior and fading may be a problem. If splicing is required, there is no choice but to steam or fuse an overlap. Test fabric stiffeners to ensure flexibility. Standard craft stiffeners must be diluted. Diluting white glue or using liquid starch are other possibilities.

FREE HANGING FABRIC

Staple or tape a fabric shade to the roller so it hangs free on top of the old shade. This is particularly helpful if you have a room darkening shade you wish to re-use. It is also a quick decorating trick for renters. Cut the fabric just a bit wider than the old shade. You may want to stiffen the fabric a bit using one of the methods listed above. Staple fabric to roller; put the shade in the window and check for straight rolling. If the fabric and

shade should not roll compatibly, you can use the fabric alone or bond it to a backing. If the two roll well together, proceed by treating side edges to prevent raveling and add a slat pocket. Each layer can have a slat, and the fabric can have a shaped and trimmed hem if desired. The pull should be underneath on the old shade.

SPLICING POINTERS

Pre-planning will eliminate problems later.

If your backing or face fabric is not long enough or wide enough, you will have to make a splice. THINK the problem through first. Chances are you can conceal the splice with some good planning.

BACKING SPLICES
Woven fabric backings such as drapery lining, may require splicing to achieve required width. Always position a backing splice crosswise, NOT lengthwise. This prevents the possibility of a streak running the full length of a translucent shade.

Plan the splice to fall (a) high on the shade where it will be rolled out of sight most of the time and/or (b) low on the shade where it will be in or behind the slat pocket.

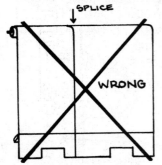
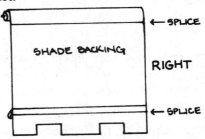

It is very important that the edges of the splice meet and overlap very slightly, about ¹⁄₁₆" - ⅛". This prevents a "dimple" or ridge on the right side of the shade. This dimple, if it occurs, cannot be removed by pressing.

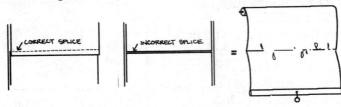

FACE FABRIC SPLICES

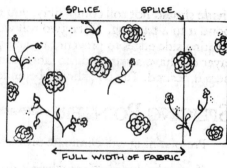

If you must splice a face fabric, the best backing choice would be a blackout type so no light would highlight the splice. Laminating glue will produce the best splice. Determine whether you might be able to turn the fabric crosswise and position the splice high on the shade, or behind the slat pocket. Sheets and double wide fabrics eliminate splicing.

If a face fabric is spliced, it is desirable to center the fabric with equal side pieces rather than placing a 'seam' down the middle.

Cut the fabric edges with smooth clean strokes using very sharp scissors, making sure the patterns match.

Preparing Fabric For Splicing

1. Lay out center panel and side pieces with fabric cut and ready for exact matching of the design.

2. Fold under the edge on one side piece until it matches the design of the center panel. Mark the center panel lightly, then cut off the excess fabric. Repeat on the other side.

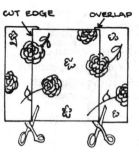

3. Place the cut edge on top of the side panel, matching the design. Using the cut edge as your guide, carefully cut through the lower layer to remove the excess fabric.

4. This leaves clean cut edges that butt together in a perfect match.

NOTE: Be sure there are no ravelings or strings that could get trapped under the fabric when it is spliced.

Iron-On Splices

Draw a guide line for the center panel and press it into place first. Then proceed with side panels. Position the edges carefully making sure they butt tightly together before you press. Avoid stretching the edges as you work. Use an up/down motion of the iron.

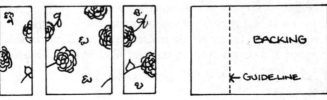

Glued Splices

Follow the general directions for bonding with laminating adhesive with the following adjustments. Draw a guideline for center panel placement.

Prepare three tubes for rolling fabric. One tube for the center panel and two shorter ones for the sides. Tape center panel in place; roll it back out of the way. Roll the side splices carefully onto the short tubes. Put glue on backing. Gently roll out the center panel aligning cut edge to guide line. Roll each side section into place carefully matching the pattern as you go. Smooth with hands, iron, let dry and continue with shade.

EXTENDING LENGTH

If fabric is a bit short for your shade, splice on an extension which would be in the 'roll-over' area or would be covered by a valance or cornice. (Also see directions for Contrasting Hem.)

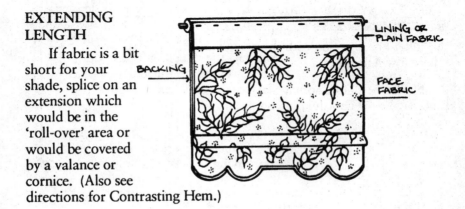

TRIM A SHADE

Here's an easy way to give an old shade a new look. Cut off the old slat hem then sew a tuck higher up. Trace on a new decorative hem treatment. Cut, then glue on one or two rows of trim, add a shade pull and your shade looks like new.

This is effective to tie a shade together with room color scheme, draperies, or window topper. Also good in damp steamy shower or tub areas where an all fabric shade might be affected by moisture. If shade will hang in a damp area—preshrinking the trim before application is advised.

CONTRASTING HEM

To tie cornice/valance and shade together use a matching hem section. Make the cornice from one fabric and the body of the shade from a second. Try reverse ground prints, print mix coordinates, stripes and dots, solids and prints, ruffles, etc. An attractive and practical method if you don't have quite enough of one fabric to do the whole shade.

Bond shade according to your chosen method. Splice on last 7"-8" in contrasting fabric. (Review Splicing Pointers)

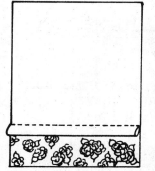

Sew or fuse the slat pocket, positioning it so the splice line is underneath the pocket where it will not show.

Finish the shade, adding slat, trim and pull. Make the coordinating cornice or valance .

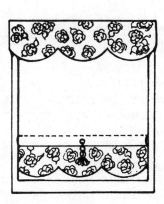

FINAL CUTTING AND MOUNTING ▬

Determine the shades finished width as follows:

Inside Brackets: Shade cloth can often be as wide as, or slightly wider than the barrel of the roller. Just so it does not rub and fray on brackets.

Outside Brackets: Usually ⅛" to ¼" from barrel ends to prevent rubbing on brackets.

Sash-run Bracket: ¼" to ½" from barrel ends to prevent rubbing on brackets or window molding.

Accuracy is critical. Improperly measured and trimmed shades may roll off center or not roll at all. Use your cardboard cutting board and carpenter's square for accurate 90° angles and straight edges.

1. Mark the long edges of the shade first using a long straight edge. Using tailor's chalk, pencil or fabric marker lightly mark the long edges. Make sure the two edges have been marked exactly parallel to one another.

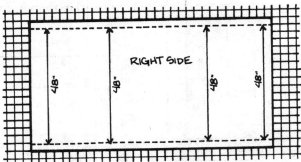

2. Carefully square and mark the short ends.

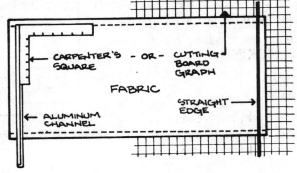

3. Cut along the marked lines with SHARP scissors, using long smooth strokes, or use a rotary cutter. Try not to lift or handle the fabric edges any more than necessary.

4. While the fabric is still flat on the work surface, slide it over to the edge of the table so it just extends over the edge. To prevent edges from raveling 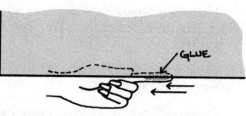 run a little white craft or laminating glue along the edge. Put a little glue on your finger, then draw the glue along the edge of the fabric, just barely touching it and leaving a small trail behind. Pat the edge gently and wipe off any excess glue as you go. Treat top and sides. Let one dry before moving on to the next.

5. The slat pocket can be sewn, glued, or bonded. If your sewing machine will not handle the bulk, or if your shade is very wide, it may be worth your while to have a shade shop or upholstery shop stitch the pocket for you. Use long basting stitches to prevent cutting the fabric and be sure the tuck is STRAIGHT. A crooked tuck makes the shade look crooked in the window.

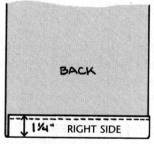

Plain Hem Edge
Turn a 1¼" tuck to the back side of the shade.

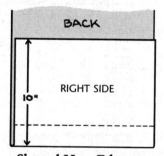

Shaped Hem Edge
Turn a 10" hem to the back side of the shade. Stitch a 1¼" tuck.

IRON-ON BACKINGS:

Plain Hem Edge

Cut a 2" strip of backing. Using a press cloth, bond the strip so it covers thefabric and makes a slat pocket. Or glue the strip in place.

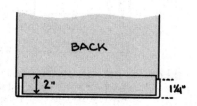

Shaped Hem Edge

Draw two parallel lines 3" apart and 7" - 8" up from bottom of shade. Use a press cloth and warm the backing with the iron to soften the adhesive, then join the lines and press in the tuck Use a press cloth and press a 1½" strip of backing across the tuck or glue the backing strip in place. Keep the strip even.

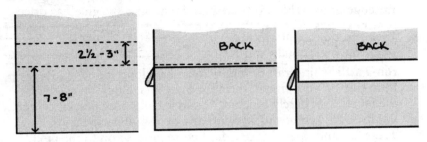

6. If you are using a shaped decorative hem edge, you have probably already selected the design — either one of your own or one from the section on Shade Trim Ideas. For more ideas look around you for guidelines in the room: the architectural features, the furnishings, etc. Arches and curves may be indicated. Is the room masculine or feminine in character? Look at the fabric itself. The design may suggest scallops, peaks, notched or looped treatment. Try to achieve a shade that will be in harmony with the room and its decor.

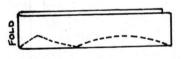

Once the design is selected, make a paper pattern. For scallops and curves use plates, saucers, platters, curved sewing rulers, etc. It is often easiest to fold a paper strip in half and work out the design. Make the strip 6" to 10" deep, and the width of your shade. Try several ideas until you are satisfied with one.

Cut the design and open the paper. You now have a balanced design.

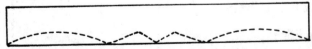

Place the pattern on the shade. Weight it or clip it so it won't move around. Trace the design, then cut it out with sharp scissors.

7. One or more rows of trim may be added to any shade style. Gimp or fringe can be glued with decorator craft glue, laminating adhesive, glue gun, or ironed on with a fusible.

   Run a bead of glue along the position of the trim, then gently press the trim in place. To help maintain sharp clean looking corners and peaks, pinch the trim between your fingers creating a raised area which can be flattened down once the glue has dried.

8. If your roller doesn't have a guideline on it, make one by placing the roller on a newspaper on a table or floor. Hold it down firmly and draw a smooth, straight line with felt pen or chalk.

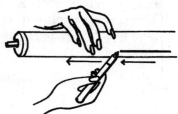

   Using the guideline, center your shade and attach it to the roller with tape or ¼" staples. Be sure you have the roller positioned correctly for reverse or conventional roll.

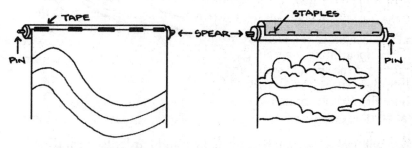

Reverse Roll   Conventional Roll

   It is very important to attach the shade straight and smooth on the roller. Test for a straight roll by picking the shade up off the table and rolling it up gently onto the roller. (If you try to roll it by pushing it along on the table you can often push it off center.) Then try it at the window in the brackets. If the shade rolls off center —

Re-position, lifting the long end slightly on the roller, and re-staple.

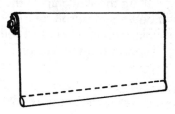

Three reasons your shade may not roll straight:
- Brackets are not level
- Window is out of square
- Shade was not cut square

9. Add a shade pull. This helps keep soiling to a minimum by keeping fingers off the shade and encourages you to pull the shade in the CENTER, the proper way to keep it on track and rolling straight. Pulls are available from shade shops, variety stores, home improvement centers, etc. Or you may make your own from macrame, stained glass, drapery rings, pottery.

SHADE TIPS

SPRING TENSION

Do not twist or attempt to adjust the spear (mechanism end) when the roller is not in its brackets. However, if a spear should get bumped and the spring tension is released, you have probably disengaged the teeth from notch (see Spearlining diagram page 125). Rewind the spring by slipping the spear through the tines of a fork. Hold the roller firmly and rotate the fork several revolutions.

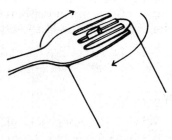

You will feel the spring become tighter and harder to turn. (Do not overwind or you can break the spring.) As spring tension increases, I sometimes grasp the roller between my knees to keep it from unwinding itself again. Now tilt the roller so the teeth catch in the spear notch and lock the spring in place.

A TOO TIGHT SPRING can be loosened by rolling the shade up to the top, taking it down and unrolling it about 6". Replace on brackets and roll it up again. Repeat until the tension is right.

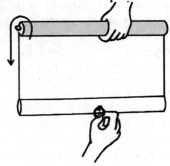

FOR A TOO LOOSE SPRING or a shade that will not roll up easily—first check the installation. If the bracket is not rubbing, bent or loose, pull the shade down about 12" and remove from brackets. Carefully roll about 6" of shade onto the roller, then replace. Repeat until the operation is smooth.

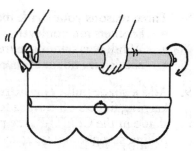

BRACKET or PIN PROBLEMS

These may be indicated if the shade falls out of the brackets or rolls with difficulty. Are the brackets straight and level? Is there 1/16" to 1/8" leeway for smooth action? Does the fabric rub against the bracket? Are brackets too far apart? The pin may be pulled out slightly to lengthen a roller that is not more than 1/4" short. If shade is rolling with difficulty, be sure pin has been put into the roller straight. When installing brackets, it is best to use screws (or plaster bolts) if possible. Nails can work loose and affect the fit of the shade.

NOTE: Never drive a nail or staple longer than 1/4" into the mechanism end. Do not oil or take metal caps off the mechanism.

SPEARLINING

When you want shades on side by side windows to stop at the same level automatically when raised, use a technique called Spearlining before you attach shades to rollers.

Lay two (or more) bare rollers down on a piece of paper. (The paper is to protect the surface so you can draw lines with felt pen, chalk or pencil.) Position the rollers so the teeth which engage the notch on the end mechanism are at exactly the same location in relation to the flat spear. Hold the rollers firmly and draw a line on the first roller. Set it aside and draw a line on the second roller, etc. The guide lines you have just drawn are now "synchronized". Attach shades to rollers along the guide lines, place in brackets at windows. The shades will now stop evenly side by side.

With a permanent marker place a mark on the wheel and the teeth of the roller. Then if the spring gets bumped or moved, you can easily re-align the shade.

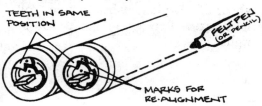

TEETH IN SAME POSITION

FELT PEN (OR PENCIL)

MARKS FOR RE-ALIGNMENT

SHORTENING THE ROLLER

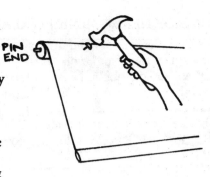

If you plan to use the same shade cloth on a roller you are shortening, roll the shade up evenly and push a tack in it at the new width. (This is the SHADE width; the roller will be longer.) Remove the tack and unroll the shade. The holes left by the tack will mark your cutting line. Before removing the shade from the roller, draw a guide line on the roller along the top edge of the shade. Remove the shade, cut to fit, then replace along line you just drew. Use tape or staples to secure the shade to the roller.

SHADE TRIM IDEAS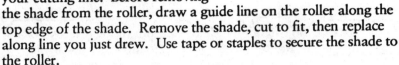

- Stencil a design or draw a design to coordinate with other fabrics in the room. This is particularly effective on a plastic or solid color custom shade.

- Applique motifs from fabric — single flowers or shapes, or strips of border trim. Glue or fuse in place. They may be stitched on if you are careful not to stretch the fabric.

- Decorative pulls can be crocheted or macramed. They may be metal or wood objects. Wood curtain rings make interesting pulls.

- Wallpaper motifs may be added to purchased shades. Glue design in the hem/border area. Do not roll up the decorated portion.

- Gimp, fringe, braid, etc. can be glued or fused to a shade border.

SHADE TRIM DESIGN IDEAS

Here are a variety of shade hem designs. Directions for making a pattern for hems are on pages 116 and 122 in Final Cutting and Mounting. These shade trim ideas can also be used for cornices and valances. Designs are usually sketched with one row of trim but two or more may be applied. Tassels may be added or removed for different effects on some designs.

SHADE HEM/CORNICE/VALANCE DECORATIVE EDGES

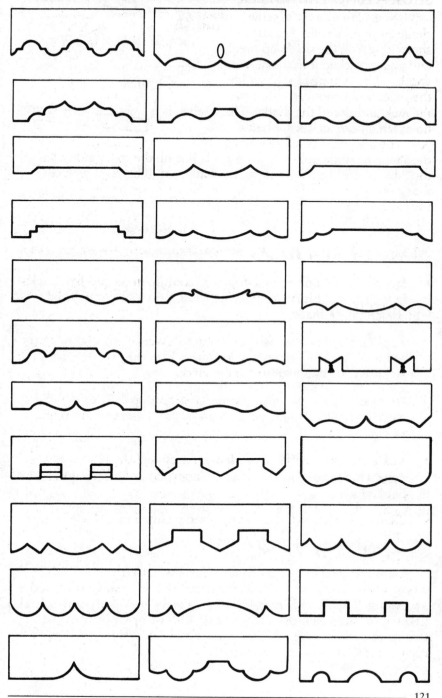

NOTE: A complete section on cornices and valances can be found in *Decorating With Fabric/An Idea Book* by Judy Lindahl.

To adapt a design for a wide shade, there are two possibilities:

- Stretch out the design, enlarging it proportionately, keeping the same number of scallops.

- Repeat more of the design — extending it at the sides. For very wide shades, this is the best method.

Basic Design #1

Enlarged by proportion, keeping the same number of scallops

Same size, sides extended.

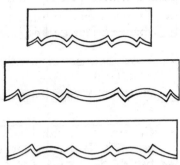

LOOP TRIM IDEAS

To determine length: Add 18" to window opening length. Laminate the shade. Turn shade back on itself and stitch two lines to form slat channel, then cut out rod straps. If desired, glue trim across front, just above cutouts. Slip rod or dowel through loops.

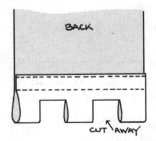

STITCHED SELF FABRIC LOOPS

Press 1¼" to back side of shade. Stitch. Make strap pieces twice the finished width and twice the finished length + ½". Cut a strip of fusible web the finished width of the strap. Center on wrong side,

STITCHED SELF FABRIC LOOPS

Press 1¹/₄" to back side of shade. Stitch. Make strap pieces twice the finished width and twide the finished length plus ¹/₂". Cut a srip of fusible web the finished width of the strap. Center on wrong side, bring edges together and fuse. Turn top and bottom edges under ¹/₄".

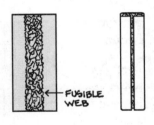

Fuse to shade, then stitch in place to slat seams as show.

Strap width and number of straps depends on width and proportion of shade.

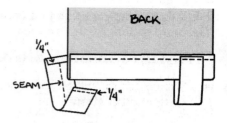

PURCHASED TRIM LOOPS

1. Turn slat hem to front side of shade. Stitch, glue or fuse.

2. Cut trim loops. Allow twice the length of loop needed, plus 2". Stitch loops to bottom front edge of shade.

3. Cut strip of trim the width of shade plus ½". Turn ends under ¼" and fuse or glue. Fuse or glue trim in place on top of slat pocket and even with bottom edge.

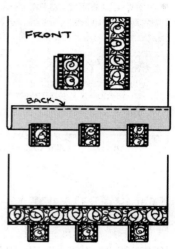

POSITIONING LOOPS AND RODS

The length and location of the rod depends on the type of bracket and mounting used with your shade.

For Inside Mount

Rod must fit inside window frame

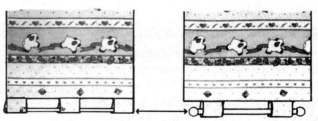

For Outside Mount

Rod ends may extend beyond shade.

Directory of Shade Brackets ▬

STANDARD INSIDE BRACKET

The most common type, used wherever there is enough depth inside a window frame to accommodate the roller. This bracket may be reversed, that is, you may place the spear bracket on the right frame and the round pin bracket on the left. You may also purchase a special reverse bracket.

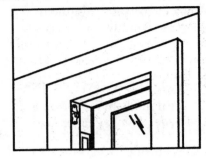

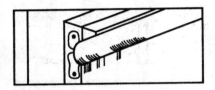
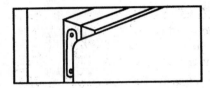

INSIDE EXTENSION BRACKET (Footless Bracket)

Mounts inside window frame. Requires less space than inside bracket. Extends slightly into room away from window. Often used for narrow framed windows, or to extend the shade outward to clear casement cranks, door hinges, etc.

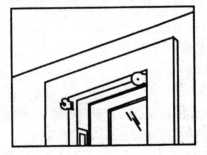

RANCH BRACKET

Clear plastic version of the inside extension bracket. Curved to follow contour of narrow, contemporary window frames.

SASH RUN (Boston) BRACKET

Special bracket for all-wood double-hung windows. Mounted at the top of the sash run (the track where the window slides up and down). Has a "bumper" to stop the window when it is raised. Mount shade in reverse roll to clear the window below.

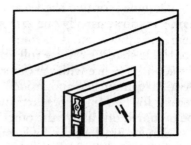

OUTSIDE BRACKET

Mounted on trim or wall adjacent to window. Used when window is not deep enough to accommodate an inside bracket. Used for shades wider than the window, to eliminate light streaks at sides, or just to give the illusion of a wider window. For wall mount use expansion bolt or anchor.

COMBINATION BRACKET

Dual-purpose brackets that hold both a window shade and a curtain rod, available in fixed or adjustable types. Eliminate the need for two sets of brackets, making a cleaner line and fewer holes in the wall.

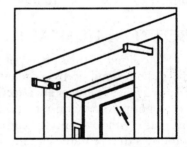

CEILING BRACKET

Very useful on ceiling-high windows, bow windows or those with deep recesses. Gives standard windows an illusion of extra height. Reverse roll recommended unless a cornice or valance covers the roller. Useful on an overhang above a window or on double-hung aluminum windows .

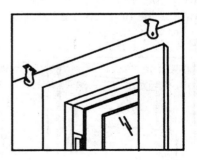

DOUBLE BRACKET

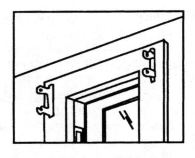

Designed for two shades at the same window, usually one is translucent, the other room darkening. The roomside shade is reverse roll to avoid interference with the other. Available in outside and inside mount (or two single brackets may be mounted one above the other).

Similar brackets can be installed at center of the window, so that one, a bottom-up shade, covers the upper sash, a regular shade pulls down to cover lower sash, permitting both windows to be opened without causing the shades to flap. Used in many schools and institutions.

HORIZONTAL INSTALLATION

For skylights, inside or ceiling brackets may be used, depending on whether the installation is within the frame or on the face of the skylight. For very large skylights, stretched wires are used to keep the shade taut. The shade is operated by a cord and pulley system similar to those in bottom-up shades.

BOTTOM-UP SHADES

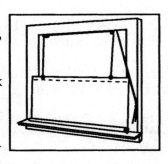

Mounted at the bottom of a window, these shades pull up by a pulley mechanism. They are especially effective when you want privacy without having to block the entire window, and for cathedral-type windows that require slanting shade tops to fit the window contour. Still-mounted or outside brackets are particularly adapted to bottom-up use.

The pulley mechanism can be attached, concealed or eliminated.

Top Mount Pulley

Sketch shows top-mount pulley with cords tied off on awning cleat, but you could also use a lock pulley, which catches and holds the cords in place like a mini-blind lock.

Slat Pulley

The cords run through the inside of a special hollow slat. This conceals most of the cord. A lock pulley is used at the top to anchor the cord at various levels.

No Pulley

Two ways to avoid pulleys and cords on bottom-up shades are:

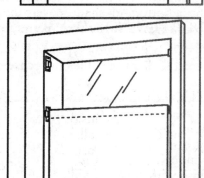

•   Shade slat to rest in brackets. Slat or rod must be longer than shade is wide. Use inside brackets for oval curtain rods, and mount them on the window frame at positions to be preferred when the shade is up. Pull shade up and set slat or rod in the brackets.

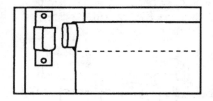

Detail of oval rod bracket.

•   Insert a spring-tension curtain rod in the hem of a bottom-up shade. This method is recommended only if shade is not raised and lowered much because the rod's rubber tips can cause worn spots on the window frame.

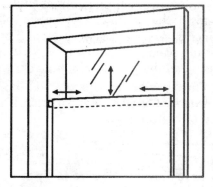

Detail of tension curtain rod.

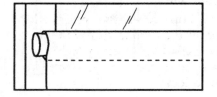

DOUBLE-HUNG WINDOW

Two sashes move up and down. Sash-run brackets are usually the choice. If you wish to light-proof the window, select outside brackets. Aluminum sash windows usually do not have enough room for inside brackets, so extension or outside brackets are often chosen.

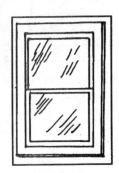

PICTURE WINDOWS

On combination types with fixed center sash and double hung, casement, or awning windows at the sides, the whole window may be treated as one; with one large shade hung from the outside or ceiling brackets. Or treat as three separate windows. If divider frames are not flush with adjacent wall, a combination of outside and footless brackets may be used to equalize the two. The outside brackets would be mounted on the divider frame, the footless brackets on jambs at either side of the window. Use reverse roll if cranks or handles are present. For multi panel windows one big shade is preferable, hung on outside or ceiling brackets, or inside brackets if there is enough room.

SLIDING WINDOWS

Usually one pane is fixed and one is movable. If set directly in plaster, use either outside or ceiling brackets. However, sliding windows set in wood sometimes give enough space for an inside or footless bracket.

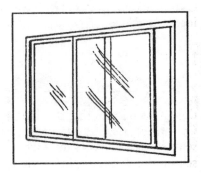

SLIDING GLASS DOORS

Whether of wood, aluminum, or vinyl, these doors and windows are handled the same. Shades may be hung from the ceiling or from outside brackets on the adjacent wall. If the latter, use reverse roll so shade clears door handle. Use one large shade or a separate one for each pane.

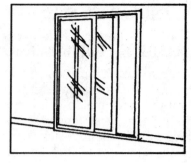

BAY WINDOW

Use separate shades for each window. Select the bracket needed according to the type of window frame and style.

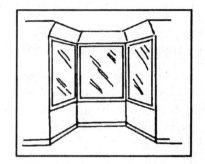

CASEMENT WINDOWS

They open like a door; at times only part of the window is movable. Mount shade so it does not interfere with handle cranks, or replace crank with a T-Handle. Use a footless bracket, or reverse roll on an inside bracket, to provide extra clearance. Use outside brackets for metal casements not deep enough for inside brackets.

BOW WINDOW

If bow is slight, one large shade may be hung straight across window area with ceiling brackets. Otherwise, treat as a bay window with separate shades for each section hung from ceiling brackets.

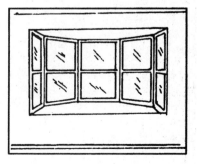

DOOR WINDOWS

French doors and half-length windows as on kitchen doors are treated alike. Shades are mounted on the door frame with outside brackets, conventional roll. Be sure shade is not so wide that it interferes with the door knob.

SKYLIGHT, STUDIO, AND DOME WINDOWS

These windows may be fitted with special installations mounted horizontally or on the slant. They are drawn with a pulley and cord mechanism.

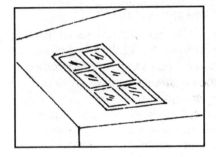

CATHEDRAL WINDOWS

Slant-top windows like these are easily handled with bottom-up shades installed at the base of the window, then drawn up from the sill on a pulley. The shade top is cut to conform to the slant of the window. If the slanted windows are above regular windows, you can use the same shade cloth—for overall unity—in a pull-down shade for the lower windows.

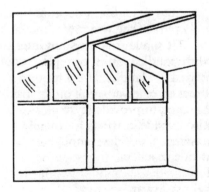

DORMER WINDOWS

These are usually deeply recessed and are best treated with inside brackets or with ceiling brackets.

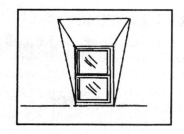

CORNER WINDOWS

One technique uses ceiling brackets. Another uses outside brackets on wall area just above windows. If the frame between windows is very narrow, there is the possibility of shade rollers interfering with each other. In this case, one shade can be hung slightly above the other and a cornice installed to conceal the irregularity. If there is no room on the inside of the window frames, shades may be hung from inside or footless brackets.

AWNING WINDOWS

These windows open to the outside and are operated by a crank or handle, which would interfere with bottom-up shades. For jalousie (top): Use outside brackets on trim, allowing clearance for the crank. For bank of awning sash (center): Use inside or footless brackets with reverse roll to allow for the crank. For fixed sash above, awning sash below (lower): Use inside or footless bracket with reverse roll to clear any projection. Bottom-up shades are especially important for these windows because ventilation is at the bottom.

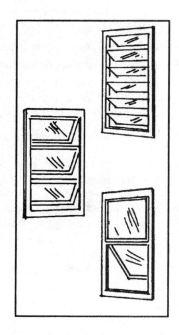

Care & Upkeep

Shades that are used often won't collect dust and grime. So the best care for all shades is simple—use them.

ROLLER SHADES
- Dust with a soft brush or use a vacuum cleaner.

- To spot clean remove shade from brackets and sponge lightly with damp cloth or treat with spot lifter.

- For more complete cleaning unroll shade on a flat surface. Wash it piecemeal using suds (like upholstery shampoo) while taking care not to abraid the surface. If needed, reverse shade—taking care not to stretch it while damp— and gently clean the back. Replace in brackets; pull down full length overnight or till thoroughly dry. Roll to top and leave rolled for twelve hours for finished well-groomed look.

- For shades that are not washable, use a wallpaper refresher.

- An art gum eraser can give many shades a quick cleaning.

ROMAN AND OTHER SHADES
- Light vacuuming or air fluffing in the dryer keeps them fresh.

- Dry cleaning is recommended over washing to prevent shrinking, stretching, distorting. Remove cords to prevent tangling.

- Cleaning in place is highly recommended.

- If you plan to wash your shades, preshrink everything before construction.

- Shades often need "dressing" to train them into the desired folding and swagging pattern. This may mean that for a while you smooth the fabric each time the shade is raised. Soon shades will develop a memory. A spray product from shade shops will also help train fabrics.

Yardage Charts

METRIC EQUIVALENCY CHART
Standard Equivalents Approved by Pattern Fashion Industry (Slightly Rounded)

Inches	mm/cm	Inches	mm/cm	Inches	mm/cm
⅛	3mm	9	23cm	30	76cm
¼	6mm	10	25.5cm	31	79cm
⅜	1 cm	11	28cm	32	81.5cm
½	1.3cm	12	30.5cm	33	84cm
⅝	1.5cm	13	33cm	34	86.5cm
¾	2cm	14	35.5cm	35	89cm
⅞	2.2cm	15	38cm	36	91.5cm
1	2.5cm	16	40.5cm	37	94cm
1¼	3.2cm	17	43cm	38	96.5cm
1½	3.8cm	18	46cm	39	99cm
1¾	4.5cm	19	48.5cm	40	101.5cm
2	5cm	20	51cm		
2½	6.5cm	21	53.5cm	**Yards**	**Meters**
3	7.5cm	22	56cm	⅛	.12m
3½	9cm	23	58.5cm	¼	.23m
4	10cm	24	61cm	⅜	.35m
4½	11.5cm	25	63.5cm	½	.46m
5	12.5cm	26	66cm	⅝	.58m
5½	14cm	27	68.5cm	¾	.69m
6	15cm	28	71cm	⅞	.81m
7	18cm	29	73.5cm	1	.92m
8	20.5cm				

SHADE CORD
FOR ROMAN, CLOUD, BALLOON, AND AUSTRIAN SHADES

SHADE LENGTH BY INCH	SHADE WIDTH 24"	SHADE WIDTH 36"	SHADE WIDTH 48"	SHADE WIDTH 60"	SHADE WIDTH 72"	SHADE WIDTH 84"	SHADE WIDTH 96"	SHADE WIDTH 108"	SHADE WIDTH 120"	SHADE WIDTH 132"	SHADE WIDTH 144"
24"	4 yds.	6 yds.	9 yds.	12 yds.	15yds.	19 yds.	23yds.	27 yds.	32yds.	37yds.	42 yds.
36"	5yds.	7yds.	10yds.	14yds.	17yds.	21yds.	25yds.	30yds.	35yds.	40yds.	46yds.
48"	6yds.	9yds.	13yds.	17yds.	21yds.	26yds.	31yds.	36yds.	42yds.	48yds.	54yds.
60"	7yds.	11yds.	15yds.	20yds.	25yds.	31yds.	36yds.	42yds.	49yds.	55yds.	62yds.
72"	8yds.	12yds.	17yds.	22yds.	27yds.	33yds.	39yds.	45yds.	52yds.	59yds.	66yds.
84"	9yds.	14yds.	18yds.	25yds.	31yds.	37yds.	44yds.	51yds.	59yds.	66yds.	74yds.
96"	10yds.	15yds.	21yds.	27yds.	33yds.	40yds.	47yds.	54yds.	62yds.	70yds.	78yds.

ROMAN SHADES

LENGTH OF SHADE	BASED ON 48" FABRIC — WIDTH OF SHADE			BASED ON 54" FABRIC — WIDTH OF SHADE		
	UP TO 40" [1 CUT]	40 1/2" TO 87" [2 CUTS]	87 1/2" TO 134" [3 CUTS]	UP TO 46" [1 CUT]	46 1/2" TO 99" [2 CUTS]	99" TO 151" [3 CUTS]
UP TO 30"	1 3/4 YDS	3 1/2 YDS	5 1/4 YDS			
30 1/2" TO 40"	2 YDS	4 YDS	6 YDS			
40 1/2" TO 50"	2 1/2 YDS	5 YDS	7 1/2 YDS			
50 1/2" TO 60"	3 YDS	6 YDS	9 YDS	BASED ON 36" FABRIC		
60 1/2" TO 70"	3 1/4 YDS	6 1/2 YDS	9 3/4 YDS	UP TO 28" [1 CUT]	28 1/2" TO 62" [2 CUTS]	62 1/2" TO 97" [3 CUTS]
70 1/2" TO 80"	3 3/4 YDS	7 1/2 YDS	11 1/4 YDS			
80 1/2" TO 90"	4 YDS	8 YDS	12 YDS			
90 1/2" TO 100"	4 1/2 YDS	9 YDS	13 1/2 YDS			
100 1/2" TO 110"	4 3/4 YDS	9 1/2 YDS	14 1/4 YDS			
FOR PATTERN REPEAT ADD ONE REPEAT PER CUT	ONE REPEAT	TWO REPEAT	TWO REPEAT			

HOBBLED (SOFT ROMAN)

LENGTH OF SHADE	BASED ON 48" FABRIC — WIDTH OF SHADE			BASED ON 54" FABRIC — WIDTH OF SHADE		
	UP TO 40" [1 CUT]	40 1/2" TO 87" [2 CUTS]	87 1/2" TO 134" [3 CUTS]	UP TO 46" [1 CUT]	46 1/2" TO 99" [2 CUTS]	99" TO 151" [3 CUTS]
UP TO 30"	2 YDS	4 YDS	6 YDS			
30 1/2" TO 40"	2 3/4 YDS	5 1/2 YDS	8 1/4 YDS			
40 1/2" TO 50"	3 1/3 YDS	6 2/3 YDS	10 YDS			
50 1/2" TO 60"	4 YDS	8 YDS	12 YDS	BASED ON 36" FABRIC		
60 1/2" TO 70"	4 1/2 YDS	9 YDS	13 1/2 YDS	UP TO 28" [1 CUT]	28 1/2" TO 62" [2 CUTS]	62 1/2" TO 97" [3 CUTS]
70 1/2" TO 80"	5 YDS	10 YDS	15 YDS			
80 1/2" TO 90"	5 3/4 YDS	11 1/2 YDS	17 1/4 YDS			
90 1/2" TO 100"	6 1/4 YDS	12 1/2 YDS	18 3/4 YDS			
100 1/2" TO 110"	6 3/4 YDS	13 1/2 YDS	20 1/4 YDS			
FOR PATTERN REPEAT ADD ONE REPEAT PER CUT	ONE REPEAT	TWO REPEAT	TWO REPEAT			

CLOUD AND BALLOON SHADES

LENGTH OF SHADE	BASED ON 48" TO 54" FABRICS — WIDTH OF SHADE				
	UP TO 24" [1 CUT]	24 1/2" TO 48" [2 CUTS]	48 1/2" TO 72" [3 CUTS]	72 1/2" TO 96" [4 CUTS]	96 1/2" TO 120" [5 CUTS]
UP TO 20"	2 YDS	4 YDS	6 YDS	8 YDS	10 YDS
20 1/2" TO 30"	2 1/4 YDS	4 1/2 YDS	6 3/4 YDS	9 YDS	11 1/4 YDS
30 1/2" TO 40"	2 1/2 YDS	5 YDS	7 1/2 YDS	10 YDS	12 1/2 YDS
40 1/2" TO 50"	2 3/4 YDS	5 1/2 YDS	8 1/4 YDS	11 YDS	13 3/4 YDS
50 1/2" TO 60"	3 YDS	6 YDS	9 YDS	12 YDS	15 YDS
60 1/2" TO 70"	3 1/2 YDS	7 YDS	10 1/2 YDS	14 YDS	17 1/2 YDS
70 1/2" TO 80"	3 3/4 YDS	7 1/2 YDS	11 1/4 YDS	15 YDS	18 3/4 YDS
80 1/2" TO 90"	4 YDS	8 YDS	12 YDS	16 YDS	20 YDS
90 1/2" TO 100"	4 1/4 YDS	8 1/2 YDS	12 3/4 YDS	17 YDS	21 1/4 YDS
FOR PATTERN REPEAT ADD ONE REPEAT PER CUT	ONE REPEAT	TWO REPEAT	THREE REPEAT	FOUR REPEAT	FIVE REPEAT

AUSTRIAN SHADES

LENGTH OF SHADE	BASED ON 48" TO 54" FABRICS — WIDTH OF SHADE				
	UP TO 24" [1 CUT]	24 1/2" TO 48" [2 CUTS]	48 1/2" TO 72" [3 CUTS]	72 1/2" TO 96" [4 CUTS]	96 1/2" TO 120" [5 CUTS]
UP TO 20"	2 YDS	4 YDS	6 YDS	8 YDS	10 YDS
20 1/2" TO 30"	3 YDS	6 YDS	9 YDS	12 YDS	15 YDS
30 1/2" TO 40"	4 YDS	8 YDS	12 YDS	16 YDS	20 YDS
40 1/2" TO 50"	5 YDS	10 YDS	15 YDS	20 YDS	25 YDS
50 1/2" TO 60"	6 YDS	12 YDS	18 YDS	24 YDS	30 YDS
60 1/2" TO 70"	7 YDS	14 YDS	21 YDS	28 YDS	35 YDS
70 1/2" TO 80"	8 YDS	16 YDS	24 YDS	32 YDS	40 YDS
80 1/2" TO 90"	9 YDS	18 YDS	27 YDS	36 YDS	45 YDS
FOR PATTERN REPEAT ADD ONE REPEAT PER CUT	ONE REPEAT	TWO REPEAT	THREE REPEAT	FOUR REPEAT	FIVE REPEAT

Simple window toppers add flair to shades and blinds. An ornate cornice doubles as a bed 'canopy'.

Photo James Seeman Studios., Div. of Masonite

Resources/Products

If you cannot locate products mentioned in this book in your local stores, the following companies can refer you to your closest retailer.

CONSO PRODUCTS CO., — Two Park Ave., NY, NY 10016, (212) 686-9890. Curtain and shade tapes, cords, hardware, trims, brackets, swag and rosette hardware, Fuse A Trim.

FUSIBLES — Steam-A-Seam® by Warm Products, Inc., Heat'n Bond® by Therm 'O Web, Stitch Witchery by HTC, Wonder-Under™ by Pellon.

GRABER INDUSTRIES, INC. — Graber Plaza, Middleton, WI (800) 356-9102. Drapery and shade hardware including Dauphine 2½" and 4", arch rods, clear rods, pinnacle 4½" D-shaped rod.

HTC, INC. — 103 Eisenhower Parkway, Roseland, NJ 07068. Fuse-A-Shade®, Fuse-A-Shade Roller Shade Kits in 48" and 60" widths.

KIRSCH — PO Box 0370, Sturgis MI 49091, (616) 651-0211, FAX (616) 651-3210. Convolute (cardboard) rollers, drapery and shade supplies including clear rods, arch rod, Continental® 2½" and 4" rods, T-handles, Velcro Rod, Swagholders, Wood poles and elbows, Kir-Flex, Mounting brackets, Weight rods.

NAKED ROOM SOLUTIONS™ (The Quick-Change Home Décor™ Company) — 4420 NW Dahlia Dr., Camas, WA 98607, Phone/FAX (360) 833-9553. Quick-Change Window Cornice Kits, Quick-Change Infinity Rings, easy decorating products, In-home Decorating Workshop, (for information on hosting a workshop or becoming a workshop coach: jsmaresh@yahoo.com.

SHADE BACKINGS — Fuse-A-Shade® by HTC, and Wonder Shade™ by Pellon.

WARM PRODUCTS, INC. —16120 Woodinville-Redmond Rd. #5, Woodinville, WA 98072, (800) 234-9276, FAX (206) 488-2630. Warm Window™ Insulating Roman Shade System, insulating fabrics, battings, magnetic tape, shade hardware and cord, T-handles, weight bars, Steam-A-Seam® fusibles in various weights, Buttoneer®.

WM. WRIGHT CO. — PO Box 398, 85 Sough St., West Warren, MA 01092-0398, (800) 628-9362. Curtain and shade tapes both traditional and transparent, cords, hardware, Magic Curtain (transparent) tapes.

MAIL ORDER CATALOGS

CLOTILDE
1909 SW First Ave., Ft. Lauderdale, FL 33315, (305)761-8655

NANCY'S NOTIONS
PO Box 68, Beaver Dam, WI 53916, (414)887-0391

THE PERFECT NOTION
566 Hoyt St., Darien, CT 06820, (203)968-1257

MISCELLANEOUS

SCOTCH WOOD JOINERS — Hardware stores. Available in several sizes. Use for cornice construction

EYELET PLIER — Fabric stores

PLASTIC SHADE RINGS — $1/2$" and $5/8$" best for Roman shades. Sold packaged or individually. Fabric, notions, knitting supplies

STAPLE GUN AND STAPLES — Fabric, hardware, craft stores

HOT GLUE GUN, LOW MELT GLUE GUN, GLUE — Hardware, fabric stores

FLOSS HOLDERS — Stitchery and notion departments

FOAM BOARD — Art and office supply. Handy for cornice construction

BUTTONEER® Fastening System — Notions Departments, Warm Products.

CORNICES — Naked Room Solutions, Conso® , E-Z, Create-A-Décor.

Index

About the Author

Judy Lindahl is a free lance home economist from Portland, Oregon. She graduated from Washington State University with honors and received her B.S. in Home Economics Education. She taught home economics in Beaverton, Oregon for several years before joining the educational staff at Simplicity Pattern Company, Inc. of New York. As an educational fashion stylist Judy traveled the country presenting programs for schools, 4-H, extension and consumer groups. In 1973 she created a program of ideas and inspiration for do-it-yourself decorators which she has presented across the U.S. and Canada. She is the author and publisher of *Decorating with Fabric/An Idea Book, Energy Saving Decorating,* and a hardback edition *Decorating with Fabric* for New Wyn Publishers (now out of print). Currently Judy teaches, travels, and volunteers. She is married to Buzz Lindahl, and mother to two daughters—Whitney and Heather. Judy has been featured in Outstanding Young Women of America and Personalities of the West and Midwest.

For more home decorating inspiration and how-tos, see *Creative Serging for the Home and Other Quick Decorating Ideas.*

For information about other Palmer/Pletsch books and products, visit our web site or call for a catalog.

Palmer/Pletsch Publishing
1801 N.W. Upshur Street, Suite 100,
Portland, OR 97209
(503) 274-0687
ORDERS: 1-800-728-3784
www.palmerpletsch.com